GLORIA

Selima Hill grew up in a family of painters in farms in England and Wales, and has lived in Dorset for the past 20 years. She won first prize in the Arvon/*Observer* International Poetry Competition with part of *The Accumulation of Small Acts of Kindness* (1989), one of several extended sequences in *Gloria: Selected Poems* (Bloodaxe Books, 2008). Published at the same time as her new collection, *The Hat* (2008), *Gloria* includes work from *Saying Hello at the Station* (1984), *My Darling Camel* (1988), *A Little Book of Meat* (1993), *Aeroplanes of the World* (1994), *Violet* (1997), *Bunny* (2001), *Portrait of My Lover as a Horse* (2002), *Lou-Lou* (2004) and *Red Roses* (2006).

Violet was a Poetry Book Society Choice and was shortlisted for all three of the UK's major poetry prizes, the Forward Prize, T.S. Eliot Prize and Whitbread Poetry Award. *Bunny* won the Whitbread Poetry Award, was a Poetry Book Society Choice and was also shortlisted for the T.S. Eliot Prize. *Lou-Lou* was a Poetry Book Society Recommendation. She was given a Cholmondeley Award in 1986, and was a Royal Literary Fund Fellow at the University of Exeter in 2003-06.

Selima Hill reads a half-hour selection of her poems on *The Poetry Quartets: 2* (Bloodaxe Books/The British Council, 1998), a double-cassette shared with Fleur Adcock, Carol Ann Duffy and Carol Rumens.

As a tutor, Selima Hill has worked in prisons, hospitals and monasteries as well as for the Arvon Foundation and London's South Bank Centre. She has worked on several collaborations with artists including: *Parched Swallows* with choreographer Emily Claid; *Point of Entry* with sculptor Bill Woodrow; and *Trembling Hearts in the Bodies of Rocks* with performance artist Ilona Medved-Lost.

SELIMA HILL

GLORIA

SELECTED POEMS

BLOODAXE BOOKS

ISBN: 978 1 85224 805 5

First published 2008 by
Bloodaxe Books Ltd,
Highgreen,
Tarset,
Northumberland NE48 1RP.

www.bloodaxebooks.com
For further information about Bloodaxe titles
please visit our website or write to
the above address for a catalogue.

Bloodaxe Books Ltd acknowledges
the financial assistance of
Arts Council England, North East.

Cover design: Neil Astley & Pamela Robertson-Pearce.

Cover printing: J. Thomson Colour Printers Ltd, Glasgow.

Printed in Great Britain by
Bell & Bain Limited, Glasgow, Scotland.

ACKNOWLEDGEMENTS

This edition includes poems selected from Selima Hill's previous books: *Saying Hello at the Station* (1984), *My Darling Camel* (1988) and *The Accumulation of Small Acts of Kindness* (1989), published by Chatto & Windus; and from these titles published by Bloodaxe Books: *A Little Book of Meat* (1993), *Trembling Hearts in the Bodies of Dogs: New & Selected Poems* (1994), [including poems from *Saying Hello at the Station*, *My Darling Camel* and *The Accumulation of Small Acts of Kindness*, together with a new collection, *Aeroplanes of the World* (1994)], *Violet* (1997), *Bunny* (2001), *Portrait of My Lover as a Horse* (2002), *Lou-Lou* (2004) and *Red Roses* (2006). The earlier title *Trembling Hearts in the Bodies of Dogs* refers to a drawing by Oswald Tschirtner, *Bebende Herzen In Liebe Der Hunde* (1979). This title, in turn, is a quotation from a poem, *Das Leben*, by Ernst Herbeck. The drawing is reproduced on page 18, courtesy of Haus der Künstler, Gugging.

A new collection by Selima Hill, *The Hat* (2008), is published by Bloodaxe Books separately from this book.

CONTENTS

FROM **Violet** (1997)

MY SISTER'S SISTER

MY HUSBAND'S WIFE

Portrait of My Lover as a Horse (2002)

O. T. 1979
BEBENDE HERZEN IN LEIBE
Der Hunde

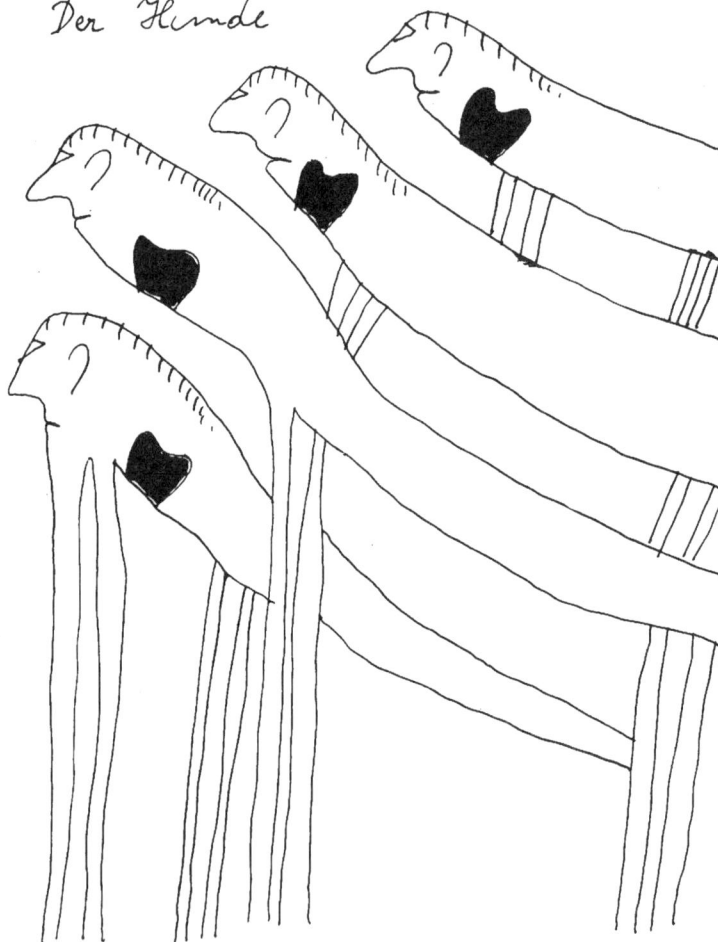

SAYING HELLO AT THE STATION
(1984)

Questioning Mr Bonnet

Mr Bonnet, the helpful Egyptologist,
explains the strange cosmology
in his *Reallexikon der ägypschen
Religionsgeschichte* that he wrote
when he was dying in Berlin:
Horus, the god of light, hid his semen
in a dish of chopped lettuce leaves,
and greedy Seth, the god of darkness,
pig-headed, metal-boned, swallowed it,
and so, by trickery, the moon was born:
Thoth, on a lotus flower, the blue baboon!

He crosses the celestial ocean
as helmsman of the world,
called Aah, the vizier of Ra, the sun.
He loads the gleaming boat
with palm leaves which record
the days and nights in notches,
for he is the measurer of time,
and he invented writing.
He carries an ivory writing palette
in his long black fingers, to instruct
the scribes who squat before him on the sand.

And he helps them on their later journey
through the Night Of A Million Years
as Thoth, the protector of the dead:
he takes them kindly by the hand
and guides them through the underworld;
his nine baboon musicians line
the long bank where the travellers
pass on their way to Osiris,
dreaming of playing draughts
with the gods and dancing with them
in the Field of Reeds.

Mr Bonnet, did you meet him, and will I,
when I step on board the silver barque?
Will he be saying *Pleased to meet you,
Mrs Hill, and how's the writing going?*
as we descend the corridors of night
into the Judgment Hall. Will he pat me
on the shoulder with his cracked

avuncular hand and, tucking my book
inside his sky-blue cape, will he wink
before he picks his tail up and climbs
onto his special perch above the scales?

Below Hekla

I appear like a bird from nowhere.
I have a new name.
I am as clean as a whistle.
I beat the buttermilk in big white bowls
until it is smooth.
I wash the pearly plates under the tap,
and fifty canvas bumpers and fifty socks.
They drip in the sun
below grey mountains like the moon's.

Each night I lift the children
in their sleep and hold out
the china pot for them:
Wilt pú pissa, elskan,
pissa, pissa I whisper
as I tiptoe from bed to bed...
Around midnight,
I go to the geyser below Hekla
and bathe in the warm water.

I am a short fat English girl.
I am twenty-five mothers.
I lead my children in a line
across the heather to the church.
The father watches me
from his dark door.
He shakes his head,
and takes me by the hand:
Blessa pú, elskan, blessa pú!

And now, September,
dust is flying: the bus is here.
I am ready.
I am on my way to Reykjavik,
Leith, Liverpool...

The children of the Barnaheimili∂
are running to the gate like hens.
Goodbye, *blessa pú*,
give our love to the Beatles, goodbye.

The Fowlers of the Marshes

Three thousand years ago
they were fowling in the marshes
around Thebes – men in knotted skirts
and tiered faïence collars,
who avoided the brown crocodile,
and loved the ibis, which they stalked
with long striped cats on strings,
under the eye of Nut, the goddess of the sky.

My mother's hushed peculiar world's the same:
she haunts it like the fowlers of the marshes,
tiptoeing gaily into history, sustained by gods
as strange to me as Lady Nut, and Anubis,
the oracular, the jackal-masked.
When I meet her at the station, I say
Hello, Mum! and think *Hello, Thoth,
This is the Weighing of the Heart.*

Dewpond and Black Drain-pipes

In order to distract me, my mother
sent me on an Archaeology Week.
We lived in tents on the downs,
and walked over to the site
every morning. It was a Roman dewpond.

There was a boy there called Charlie.
He was the first boy I had really met.
I was too shy to go to the pub,
but I hung around the camp every night
waiting for him to come back.

He took no notice of me at first,
but one night the two of us
were on Washing-Up together.
I was dressed in a black jersey
and black drain-pipes, I remember.

You in mourning? he said.
He didn't know I was
one of the first beatniks.
He put a drying-up cloth
over my head and kissed me

through the linen BREEDS OF DOGS.
I love you, Charlie I said.
Later, my mother blamed herself
for what had happened. *The Romans
didn't even interest her*, she said.

Elegy for the Bee-god

Stingless bees
were bred in tree hollows
for beeswax and honey.
Every year, in the month
called Tzec, the bee-keepers
played their raspadores
and danced across the fields
with bells and ribbons
round their feet, to honour
the fat bee-god, who buzzed
in the heated air
to their music.
He lived in a gold house
in the hotlands, and drank
cocoa sweetened with honey.

All's quiet now, it's June,
and he's not here, the late,
the long-forgotten bee-god,
who sped on zigzag wings
across the sky to the faithful.

Cross-eyed, bejewelled
and tattooed, drumming
his fluffy yellow feet
on the tree hollows,
he gave the bees new hope,
and cocoa sweetened with honey.

If ever I find him – thin,
justly offended, dead
in the dry chaparral –
I will put jade beads
and honey on his tongue,
and wrap him in a shroud
of wings, and loop his neck
with pearls from Guatemala;
I will light him candles
of beeswax, bringing sleep,

and he will rest in the shade
of the First Tree,
and wait for me there –
humming a tune, and drinking
cocoa sweetened with honey.

A Voice in the Garden

Gerald's here! my mother called,
Are you ready? The taxi was waiting
to take us to our weekly swimming lessons.
I drove through Marylebone like a V.I.P.
our kind neighbour close beside me,
smelling of soap and peppermint...
He squatted on the edge of the pool
and shouted *One, two! One, two!* as I struggled
with the water like a kitten. I kept my eyes
on the gold buttons of his blazer.
They were as smooth and glossy
as the boiled sweets he liked to suck,
and offer to his young friends.
I sank and kicked and spat out water.
The bright buttons rose and fell...

And then one day he came in beside me,
his old grey body quaking
like a mollusc without its shell.
The wet wool of his bathing trunks
reminded me of blankets I had peed on.
His hands in the moving water
seemed to float between my legs.
He smiled. I swam to the edge of the pool
and pulled myself over the steps.
The heated water trickled down my legs
as I wrapped my towel round me like a shawl.
That was our last swimming lesson,
but he still came to tea on Sundays,
after his 'little siesta',
and sat down in the seat next to mine.

As he listened to my mother –
picking his biscuits off his plate
with pink eager fingers, lifting
his tea-cup to his lips, and nodding –
he pressed a silver florin in my hand.
I kept them in a muff in my drawer,
under my uniform. At last I poured them
into a little plastic bag and took them by bus
to the Little Sisters of the Poor
in Albert Street... Next Sunday, I hid
in the garden, but he came pushing his way
through the roses, looking for me.
I heard the twigs breaking up, and his voice
in the bushes calling and calling –
Yoo-hoo, Gerald's here, you-hoo...

The Ram

He jangles his keys in the rain
and I follow like a lamb.
His house is as smoky as a dive.
We go straight downstairs to his room.

I lie on his bed and watch him
undress. His orange baseball jacket,
all the way from Ontario,
drops to the floor – THE RAMS, in felt,

arched across the hunky back.
He unzips his calf-length
Star-walkers, his damp black Levi's,
and adjusts his loaded modelling-pouch:

he stands before me in his socks –
as white as bridesmaids,
little daisies, driven snow.
John Wayne watches from the wall

beside a shelf-ful of pistols.
Well, he says, *d'you like it?*
All I can think of is Granny,
how she used to shake her head,

when I stood by her bed on Sundays,
so proud in my soap-smelling
special frock, and say *Ah,
Bless your little cotton socks!*

The Diving Archaeologists

Led to the Sacred Well of Sacrifice
by the ancient peculiar map
of Diego de Landa, the archbishop,
here in the hot jungle,
where temples sink in mud,
he decides to send for Paterson,
the diver, who is gathering sponges
off the Bahama Islands.

26

Bound virgins, carrying jade
and chipped obsidian to appease
the glittering serpents,
were thrown into the well
by singing priests at daybreak –
fair female appellants
sent to talk to the goddess
and reason with her under water.

The divers, weighted by their new
iron shoes and necklaces of lead,
are let down into the well
by native boys, who are crying.
The air-valves go pht! pht!
as the waters close
and the light rays
change to purple.

Sunk on ledges, in soft
gruel-thick mud, they find
drowned women's bones, and nodules
of yellow perfumed resin,
and the presents of jade
and obsidian, carefully
broken by the priests
to release their sacred spirits.

When the divers surface,
trailing slimy loops of weed
like hair, their helmets
bump against the bottom of the raft.
The native boys throw down
their wide bleached hats
in fear, and call out
on the swaying pontoon:

El Amo! The Master!
In her anger, the goddess
has swallowed him,
and now she comes knocking,
as a warning – we must not
go down where the women hold
their secret meetings,
in the Well of Chichén Itzá.

The Flowers

After lunch my daughter picked
handfuls of the wild flowers
she knew her grandfather liked best
and piled them in the basket of her bicycle,
beside an empty jam-jar and a trowel;
then, swaying like a candle-bearer,
she rode off to the church
and, like a little dog, I followed her.

She cleared the grave of nettles
and wild parsley, and dug a shallow hole
to put the jam-jar in. She arranged
the flowers to look their best
and scraped the moss from the stone,
so you could see whose grave
she had been caring for.
It didn't take her long – no longer
than making his bed in the morning
when he had got too old to help her.

Not knowing how to leave him,
how to say goodbye, I hesitated
by the rounded grave. *Come on,*
my daughter said, *It's finished now.*
And so we got our bicycles and rode home
down the lane, moving apart
and coming together again,
in and out of the ruts.

Ty-Coch

And now the snow has fallen
over the house where we were lovers
and the weight of the snow
has made the roof cave in.

They have taken away the timbers,
and put the bed out on the terrace
where the roses used to grow.
Snow surrounds the house

in drifts, like bears;
and sheep, come down off the mountain,
shelter in the room
we used to love in.

Chicken Feathers

I

What a picture!
She has tucked her wild-looking chicken
under her arm and stares out
over what seems to be a mountain pass
on a windy day.
She is wearing a blue linen dress
the colour of summer.
She reminds me of Brunhilde – alone, bronzed, unfamiliar.
She doesn't look like anybody's mother.

II

She used to love dancing.
She went to the Chelsea Ball
dressed as a leopard;
there she met my father,
who looked so dashing
in the Harlequin suit
his tailor made for him
from raw silk.
He had tiny shoes
like Cinderella's.
I have seen them.

III

She comes to collect me from school,
on time, silent,
and I hand her my coat and satchel –
avoiding, even then, her lovely eyes,
that look down on my world
like distant stars.
I play with the girl next door,
and don't come home till bed-time.

IV

From the lighted window
I watch my mother
picking leeks in the twilight.

I will have soup
for my supper,
sprinkled with parsley.

She passes me my creamy bowl.
My hands are warm,
and smell of soap.

My mother's hands are cold as roots.
She shuts up the chickens
by moonlight.

V

How can they think I am asleep
when he bends down and kisses
the nape of her neck,
and goes away to his own room,
while she sits in front of her mirror
and brushes and brushes
her waist-long silver hair?

VI

The hens are all gone.
How happy she used to be
setting out in her long tweed coat
across the orchard
with her bucket.
Chuck, chuck, chuck, she called
and they'd all come running.

VII

She walks behind the hedges
of the large garden, stooping
from time to time
to pick narcissi
for her mother's grave,
now that it is Easter.
We don't want to go.
We're too young to remember
our grandmother –
and besides it will be cold
in the grave-yard
where the wind blows
straight in off the downs.

VIII

He went to his room with an orange
in his hand, and died there
sometime during the afternoon.
My mother spent the day in the kitchen.
When I came in from the garden
I was sent upstairs
to call him down to tea:
he was sitting by the window
with his back to me.
On the table beside him
were four boats made of orange peel,
with the pith piled neatly inside them.
My mother couldn't stand up.
She kept on saying she was sorry,
but she couldn't stand up.
It must be the shock she said.
It wasn't grief.
Come and sit down she said,
And have your tea.

IX

Tonight I kissed my mother,
for the first time that I can remember;
though I must have kissed her before,
as all daughters kiss their mothers.
She was passing in front of me
to kiss the children, and I leant down
and touched her cheek with my lips.
It was easy – like the lighting of a candle.

X

My sister always says
that on the morning our father died
he was working on a drawing of a liner
disappearing over a white horizon.
She says it is a symbol.
She's got the picture by her bed.
I would rather think of dying
as a coming into harbour,
a sort of final mooring.

XI

You put in at a little jetty.
There is someone there to welcome you –
not sinister – but rather surprising –
someone you know. In front of you rise
banks of fern and shining celandines.
You can smell the woods.
They are full of life,
but very still.

XII

My mother and I, in our way,
understand each other.
When I kneel by her grave,
in need of a little consolation,
I will picture her standing
on a hillside in bright sunlight,
lifting her hand to wave to me;
or is she brushing away the feathers
that drift like dreams into her hair
and tickle her cheek, till she smiles?

MY DARLING CAMEL

(1988)

The Holidaymakers' Daughter

It doesn't matter what she looks like.
She's in one of her moods again,
and her parents, God bless them,
have driven off in their old Ford,
leaving her alone
on a rock overlooking the sea,
with the key to the bungalow,
in case it starts to rain,
and something to eat
in the fridge.
It doesn't matter, her mother had said,
but her father was red as a beetroot.

She will uncurl in her new-found solitude
like paper flowers from Japan
that grow when you put them in water.
She will develop
a kind of passionate detachment,
like a hen. (At night she reads
The Elegant Sayings of the Lamas –
'a hen when at rest produceth
much fruit', that sort of thing.
She tries not to see the hen
too literally, but to get a feeling
of purity and earnest calm.)

Father Biddy, The Horse-Guard Priest –
who was he, she wonders,
with his shaven head and long black skirts
and his grey that he galloped at dawn?
She did know one priest, Father John.
He visited the Pet Cemetery
when she was doing the flowers,
but he was fat, and holding his hand
was like holding a helping of trifle.
He hid pennies in his habit
and asked the girls to find them.
She couldn't learn peace of mind from him...

I need a father, she concludes,
who would find it perfectly natural
to roll my body into a ball
and leave me in peace in a sandy cave
like the mummy of Uan Muhuggiag...

She's just nodding off on her warm rock,
a neat furry bundle
smelling of aniseed and myrrh –
not 'unfurling' at all,
or feeling 'nice to live with' –
when she hears the Ford
backing into the lane,

and picks up her binoculars
as if she's watching the birds.

The Significance of Significance
(i.m. Dorothy Richards)

She was worried he couldn't be happy
just loafing about by the river,
like she liked doing.
Plans, and plans about plans, and sex,
was *his* idea of happiness.
He wore a floppy hat.
She felt so lonely!

Another thing, she couldn't spell.
Laborinth. Itiniry. Elann.
She cooked him cockles
in a thick orange sauce,
and bought him a suitcase –
'for the Great Man'.

They sat on a rocky mountain
dressed in leather.
Sardines and beer.
Parois vertigineuses.

Their children were his books.
She understood that.
O Significado De Significado,
lecture notes.

'The blissfully well-run nursing-home'
is now public knowledge –
her little lump, like longing,
prized from her oesophagus;
her crawling from the hut
on her knees.

A tortoise-shell comb,
embroidery,
The Crack.
A lovely moth.
'The nurse is a crashing bore'
...poking about among her mysteries.
God bless you, Patty.

Queenio

Sand the risen peach, swollen with lust,
introduce a finger-nail tentatively
under its congested lip;
the juice will coil down her wrists
and lonely open hips, restless,
engorged with maggots. *Please come home.*

Lust has turned her hidden milk to bone.
Peach-blossoms stiffen,
goat-thick orchards sink,
eyed beetles wink and push like hounds
against her skin; *peach-girl, don't go.*
Shaky, untouchable, defiled by desire,

she casts around for somewhere soft to lie.
Come here. The knee-deep fruit play Queenie
with her loving soul, stripped clean
and tranquil by the coloured mouths
of peaches soft as eiderdowns.
They whisper *Queenio.* I said *Come here.*

Peggy

He loved the sunlight –
this was in New Mexico –
he loved the sunlight,
and he used to go for long walks
with the llama, Peggy;

and when his mother died,
one night in June,
he brought the llama with him
to the funeral:
standing like a queen in the mist,

batting her long eye-lashes
like cream.
His mother died
to get away from them!
She suffered terribly.

He used to be a tailor
like his father –
pricking his pot-belly with the pins
and sucking the redcurrants
that he made.

His mother was a gold statuette.
He wanted so much love,
that was the trouble,
yet, if you tried to smile,
he looked away.

The llama called him
Chocolate Eyes.
She said, *Don't cry.*
She was the only thing
he wanted in the end.

Natural Wonders

I

The lovely boy
washes himself all over

in a ski-hut. His mother sends
a new suit every year.

'He only cares about
his mathematics.'

II

He's tired.
He hates the snow.
He can't stop masturbating.

Each little death,
each floating point cries
Heaven, where are you now?

III

The handsome mountain-dwelling monk lies dead.
Something is wrong with the electric fan.

His secret love-affair
exceeds his wildest dreams,

while here on earth
the other monks are lapsing.

NOTE: *In the technical term 'decimal floating point', the sequence 2658 13, for example, would be used to represent the number 7.658 x 1013, or 26580000000000.*

Lotty

A white South African depressive
is kneeling on the veldt in Waterberg
training the beam of an electric torch
onto a little garden, where a king and queen
in white are watering their fungi-beds.
Baby soldiers wriggle on the paths,
and lift their heads from time to time
to suck the lovely globules forming
on the queen's black jaws...

He kneels by the nursery all night.
It's true he isn't well.
His wife died, and he lived alone
with Tame Toktokkie X and Tame Toktokkie Y.
His six-inch mother scorpion,
who carried sixteen babies on her back
in pairs, died recently as well.
He used to call her Lotty, or Carlotta,
his mother's and his grandmother's name.

Lucy

They lie down naked in the spider room
where legs are ears. They listen as they spin.

Then Lucy takes him for a walk. My dear,
in half an hour, she is in love with him.

Ulrike Meinhof, sing angelically;
Mongol invaders, bathe in padded light;

it is the Buddha passing on his elephant.
Lucy, take your love and follow him.

Benjamin

I am so close
I could kiss you, Benjamin.
(Our eyes never meet.)
Do you remember
slicing shins like fruit?

Do you remember
stepping through the snow
with nothing on?
(I'm pulling off your jeans.
I'm very close.)

You dance and hide
and live on peas
like necklaces.
(She wishes you would smile,
but you don't.)

You're sleeping on the floor
beside your *ra*
where crow-black songs
revolve, revolve, revolve.
(Your mummy thinks you are a sort of ghost.)

A Skiing Accident

Even the humble mole
dreams while he sleeps,
a little man as clean as a tomato.
Lives in hills, dreaming of a beetle coming in.

The presidents
dream of the presidents,
breaking their hearts on the piste.
Pineapple Lip Balm. Blood on her mitts.

The Seashore House

The sound of waves
comes creeping through the house
to stroke the sullen waters
of the garden, and my body,
like a stone, beside the garden,
begging, begging to be left untouched,
because she's bruising me:
may all her slow attempts
at getting close to me
fly off into the sound of waves
like birds with rock-grey wings!
I lie as still as someone
balancing a bowl of fruit
or rabbits on their head.

Beside the pond my dog
is gnawing bones
that crawl with ants,
and every now and then he stops
to rub his lips and nose
along the grass
that closes over him.
This afternoon aches
like a bell,
the sea is slow,
and if you come and look for me
beside the pool of melted water
you will find a stone
as cold and passionless as silk.

Silk is the liquid stone
my mother wore,
I see it slipping, slipping, like a skin;
I wear a scarf myself sometimes, I know,
to hide the scar
my mother made
I do not want to show:
my mother is afraid of love
and I, her silver-skinned
burnt only daughter –
tissue-head, peculiar, queen of pain –
I cry for kisses like she cries for shame.
The sound of waves
comes creeping through the house.

Early Nights

When people asked her
what her secret was,
she always answered
Early Nights.

She came upstairs
before I was asleep myself
sometimes, wearing a pair
of blue silk pyjamas.

I couldn't get to sleep
because the thought of silkworms
making silk in little boxes
gave me nightmares.

We had a magic word –
Przewalski
Przewalski –
to make them go away.

Przewalski was a captain
who was mad about Mongolia,
and trained wild horses
to 'die' for him.

Darling,
she used to say,
if praying doesn't work,
imagine visiting the zoo:

feel the lovely elephant,
the antelope, the gnu.
They sleep by the canal.
Recite their names.

It never works.
The captain
is a cruel man,
and I can't pronounce his name.

The Unsuccessful Wedding-Night

It's all because of Buster.
Of course, it's unreasonable,
he couldn't possibly have come –
his barking, his midnight walk,
the way he scratches at the blankets –

but as she presses her face
into the pillow of the small hotel,
she can't help missing him
terribly. She imagines the two of them
hiking in bright sunshine

over the Western Ghats; and soon
she begins to whimper to herself,
her runny nose trailing
over the foam pillows
like the Vasco da Gama of snails.

The Ptarmigan Hunter

I

I'm being kept awake
by too many kisses

and the new central-heating system
of a high-rise Carousel hotel.

The hot pipes go *tick tick*
and this man I hardly know

keeps turning me over and over
like the hunter on the radio

who came across a mummy
while on holiday in Greenland.

II

Lady of Qilakitsoq,
sleeping on ice,

your face tattooed
by the old woman

with the seal-bone needle,
your body wrapped

in cormorant skins
and polar willow leaves,

sleep
while you can.

III

An off-duty ranger
drove over in his Dodge from Umanak

to shoot ptarmigan,
and found a young woman, freeze-dried,

like coffee, under a rock.
He cut off her black underclothes

and took them home to his father
who, being afraid of ghosts,

fed them into the Garbage Guzzler
he had just bought.

The Bath

He presses an oval of soap
into the palm of his hand
and twirls the bristles in the violet foam

until it quilts his fingers like the snow
where trappers crawl to pull the hairs
from little Russian weasels.

I lie under the greying water; drape
my flannel on my curls
like palls, or like the coloured coats

that poodles wear; or muslin
lain on cheese in dingy larders
to protect it from the flies.

Not that he's likely to look:
his only joy's his – twizzle twizzle twizzle –
obsessive pirouettes. Then I remember

He's been dead for weeks.
I roll over in the water thoughtfully,
feeling – not lonely exactly –

more like a floating pear-half
having warm chocolate sauce poured over me.

Mother Stone

My father was a tall man who approved of beating,
but my mother, like a mother stone,
preferred us to be sitting in a small room
lined with damson-coloured velvet
thinking quietly to ourselves, undisturbed;
everything was slow and beautiful
when we were being punished: all we had to do
was watch the dark-red petals' roses
press against each other in a slight breeze
on the window pane, and blossoms fall
in silence from the cherry tree;

and now my son is lying in a long white shirt
across our eiderdown, trying to stay awake,
and fingering my spine's shell pink as if I were a beach
and he were blades of marram grass in drifts of sand.
I dab my face with cream that smells of cucumber
and whisper in a distant milky voice
Of course I'll wake you up when he comes;

and then his eyelids close,
and in his self-created darkness he is following
a big car on a motorway at night,
it turns into the driveway to the house,
and presently the driver gets out:
it is only a bear in the moonlight,
walking on the lavender beds.

Eating Chocolates in the Dark

And after that, the diaries stop.
We think he went to his grandmother's,
whom he adored apparently.
They sat on her bed
with the lights turned off,
and ate chocolates,
and listened to the sea.
It was a kind of ritual
they both found very comforting.
Her other love was hyacinths.
He said he didn't like them,
and asked her to take them away.

And then he started telling her
about a lost eskimo
who paddled up the Don in a kayak.
He was dressed in sealskin,
and very tired. After a few days,
he caught a cold and died.

The dip dip dip of the little boat,
and his sad story-telling voice,
were like a lullaby,
and she was asleep, or nearly asleep,
when suddenly he asked her
if she believed in God.
(She told me all this quite openly –
the old Russian grandmother,
half lying back on her cushions.

Perhaps I shouldn't say this, she said,
but listen to me for a moment –
if you wake up,
and feel something fat like a puppy
wriggling between your legs,
you're not going to say it's God,
or the answer to all your questions,
or Love, are you? It's sex!
It was the same for him.)

No one

No one is to touch me
but the Lord.

His fingertips caress me
like a knife.

Everywhere I go
I am adored.

I want to be a monk
but I'm a wife.

Not All the Women of England

At the top of the bank
a blond airman
is doing sit-ups
in the tenderest
of early-morning sun.
I want to squash him flat.
He's like my Uncle Pat's
gold cigarette-case
that flies open
when you touch it.

You cruise along the fence
with your elbow
on the rolled-down window-edge.
*Everything you come near
falls to bits.*

The cattery sells bedding-plants
and runner-beans.
Someone has been up here
to mow a tiny lawn,
and hang a sign above it,
opposite the fence I mentioned
and the bank, before the airman came.

The passenger, the passenger,
I don't want to be the passenger.
Please can we stop at the Trout Lakes.

You came into my bedroom
carrying a duck,
and we lived together happily
for five years.

(She was so tame,
they wrote about her
in the *Whitby Gazette*.)

And now you're driving a saloon
I've come to hate
round and round the camp
like a bum.
I think I'm going to say
I want to leave you.
I want to leave you.

The hearts on the shutters
make the houses look like
cuckoo-clocks, or little chalets –
can you hear the cow-bells tinkle? –
where Mother Bear and Father Bear
eat fondue. They overlook
the fence and the bank.

The airman walks away
to living-quarters
we can't see
like a zoo animal.

He polishes his boots.
He's far from home.
Deep in trout lakes on the other side
trouts' dreams of flies
come true...

Not all the women of England
are boiling kettles
by the tall gates
but I love them all.
They shelter in the oaks
on the soft verges
where the airman lights up
his king-size cigarette.

Jacko's Girl

Send me a real dog-faced ape
that rides a dog, and plays the harp
or lute, who goes 'la la la la'
and stands up upside-down in the park.

We'll walk round flower-beds,
through rooms of light,
looking for the room I fell in love in,
singing *Stella Maris* in my bra.

That's where the velvet monkey lived.
I wanted him. I saw his dark red fingers
crush his dress.
He was my sister Mary's doll, not mine.

My present was my first geranium,
that smelled of peppermints and had no bones.
It was a post. I wanted a baboon.
They come from Abyssinia in crates.

Ouarzazate

Flies are entering
my mouth.
They drink
at my eyes.
They love them.

I've lost my hands
so how can I
brush them away?
C'est toujours midi,
Madame.

My heart goes
boom pause boom pause boom.
Don't touch me,
je vous en prie,
or I'll kill you.

Visiting the Zoo

The tall giraffes can never sit.
Their names are Valerie and Gwendoline.

I am their tall reticulated son.
This is our sand and hay.

Follow our gold strip to holy Tassili,
blonde swallow-tails, hares, a little milk.

You are a good girl. He will never know
you are in love with someone else, not him.

The Small-Mammal House

My twin sister Mary leans against a cage
where little kinkajous are watching her with interest.

Arboreal nocturnal sort of bears
with a passion for your chocolate, I see.

All I got was bits of chewing-gum –
your 'sapodilla-gum-tree-juice-gum', chickle.

Who took the photo anyway?
You shouldn't let them when you look like that.

'*Glissez, mortels, n'appuyez-pas*, GLISSEZ !'
Remember Louli, with her ear-muff hair?

'Tippy-toes, tippy-toes, tall as you can!
Reach up to those forbidden chocolates, Mary!'

You were my elective mute, becoming almost elegant
in time to Louli's elevating music...

It isn't good to watch small mammals by the hour,
all hunched-up. Also, funny men go down there, Mummy said.

Parrots

I am surrounded by parrots.
They leave their chopped tomatoes on my head.
They pile at my feet like dying socks.

Their lettuce-coloured shoulders are so heavenly
the people at the zoo go mad about them.
One of them is looking in my eyes,

and saying, *What's the matter, Billy?* (meaning me).
Catch them, someone, take them back to Paradise,
they're giving me a terrible disease.

Looking for Camels

She followed him all afternoon,
although he didn't speak to her,
or even turn to watch her
climb the dusty road.
White moths settled on her feet.
She saw a mule
with ants inside its ear.
M'sieur, m'sieur, the children cried,
running through poppies
with silver knives... Boar droppings.
Snake country... *Of course I know*
exactly where we are.

He walked into the mountains
like a man who's on his way
to kill a dog. He didn't stop.
She closed her eyes to let a drop
of calamine run down her cheek.
Somewhere sandy, somewhere soft,
that's what he had promised her...
She wrote a letter home in her head:
There's nothing here but rock,
she began,
and his HI-TEC HI-TEC HI-TEC
footsteps in the snow.

Devotion

I

My darling camel,
I want to tell you very clearly
I feel normal.
All those years of coming here
in black with P. are over.
Say you're interested.
You're so disdainful!

II

Phlegmatic, waterless, you trot,
but sometimes pace, like bears.
Deaf goats and hens
climb up and down your neck.
We ship and slaughter you.
We drink your blood.

III

I spent the days in boxes
keeping quiet.
The blue fish on the cushions
were my friends.
And during all that time
I didn't come.

IV

And then one day, my darling,
I was your *freshly-washed injected devotee*.
I stood beside your moat
with my nurse.

V

Please kiss me with your flaccid lips.
Roam free. Sweet waters of the dayas, rise.
Your feet are like an ostrich's.
You carry gold in goat-skin water-bags.
You carry brides.

VI

At sunset, I go home with the zoo-man.
His hands are like enormous teddy-bears.

THE ACCUMULATION OF
SMALL ACTS OF KINDNESS

(1989)

The Accumulation of Small Acts of Kindness

Italics are used here for the imaginary voices the diarist hears in her head; double quotation marks for the direct speech of doctors, visitors, etc; and single quotation marks for indirect speech or words she reads or remembers reading.

PART ONE

The In-Patient

CHAPTER 1 **Boys**

Whatever's the point of writing it all in code?
Supposing the coat is a monk,
and the sofa's a young horse;
and supposing the photos are real?
Darling, I love you.

I want to stay here in the dark for ever.
Everyone, don't talk and move around.

'A strange lamented artist who loves dancing.'
Somebody's clock. I hate her. Cold white lines.
Cut light in concave triangles, the door,
the side of the door, the panel's lonely back.
I think I am a sponge. I think I'm going.
Or shall I write in code again? Who cares.

She was descending like a boneless swan.
I wish more people would descend like that.
She knows I'm writing about her. Now she's gone.
Mr C. is calling. Here I am,
hidden in my wooden hold of doors.
Last night G. told me everything. It's true:
I will always remember you, G., I really will.
I wanted to tell you about...I nearly did.

She asked me if I masturbate. Wet grass.
Hepburn – 'fragile, feminine' – please die.
Rays of light returning on themselves.
Glossy prints of Rudolf Nureyev.

Taut purity of virgins in white landscapes,
overwhelmed by tenderness.
Don't go.
"Like drugs –" he said, "the same basic principle."
'Rebellion itself's a form of love.'

Obsession with counting birds.
My lips are aching.
They have taken away my Lord.
The Head is calling.

Marine crustaceans' seven leg-like mouths.
Goodwin's MOODS AND TENSES. Pipe tobacco.
'Little did the author know.'
Plisetskaya.

I wonder if I'm good at telling lies.
'Un homme secret, il danse dans la rue.'
I do not know the rules.
Oh yes you do!

"What's she really like?"
She is a virgin.
Yellow parrots, lettuce, nylon wool.
I went back to the study after supper.
The bluebells are in session in the woods.
Wearing dresses frightens me.
Calves.
Nipples.
The teachers smell of beans and dressing-gowns.

The dark proud gentleness of feathers
reflected in the dancer's famous face.
Her hair is gold. She hates the other partner.
Black satin, tinsel, armaments unfold.
She didn't know she made me cry. I told her.
Broad hands. Dark blood. A little rice and milk.
Down down down to the creator
of diamonds and coal and roots in silver tights.
Beaten cut tormented killed and counter-killed.
This isn't what you think. It's radioactive.
Many men and unknown things go down there.
Won't write about the walk. Past. Frozen colour.

Noises echo through the whitened squares.
'Mauriac choisit Emmanuelle.'
Hiding during meals – the seventh day.
I won't be watched so much by people later.

'Slowness Is Beauty' – always at top speed.
"I simply came to see if you're alright..."
'Suppressed depression, iron will' – that's me!
"You'll burn your journal next year – DEFINITELY."
Her fatherland. Tormented hope. Horned tree.

'Albert Schweitzer – famous bearded saint,
authority on Goethe and musician.'
'A policeman drags away a limp protester.'
'It is difficult to assess how far the jazzman
"sends" himself in the course of any session.'
The best thing they could do is to invent
a nice white dye that they could dye us with.
'Early evening in Trafalgar Square –

police begin their long removal job.'
MYSTERY MAGAZINE. I want a letter.
Writing a list of the people I have kissed – no,
writing a list of the people who've kissed me.

I have not been in Hall for eighteen days.
Chicken, peaches, cheese.
I don't know why.
'Some of the young Germans taking part
rebuild the vestries of the old cathedral.'
I want to go to B. The grass is shining.
Why do I write his name? It isn't true.
I threw the chocolate biscuits in the bushes.
Everyone is eating.
G.'s in tears.
It is not *God* who must be good and kind.
Patients eat in teams.
The rivers wind.

My socks are blood-soaked.
Gradual shapeless gloom.
I've dreamt of it three times.
White grapes for supper.
I took them all outside.

Nobody saw.
Running when exams are over.
Paris.
I'm going to eat outside again tonight.
Frosted hay. The smell of chives and boots.
I will be sixteen in the night.
My poetry.
I want to wash my hair.
I think she's looking.

H. has got a photo. I will steal.
It's all because of H. I told you so.
Everything she's got I want.
I'll scream.

Copulation in the form of memories.
Attempts in parents' bedroom.
Cockle-shells.
'Sensible comme les bouchers.'
Banded snails.
Boys in leather jackets wait for girls.
I want it. Knees like huts. *I want it I want it.*
The Bishop of Wool. His gracious reality. Nuts.

"This doubling back she mentions seems to be
the most dynamic and influential sensation":
the door is for a long moment opened –
the timeless curling motion – sand and toes…
All I can write is *Love me love me love me.*
The unforgettable dream. The golden sand.
The unforgettable dream, already forgotten.
All I can write is gathered in my hand.

He was kissing a different woman every time.
I don't know how to laugh. *Hilarious laughter.*
'Dans le petit berceau peint en blanc,
il attendra le retour de Belmondo.'
Still telling me I write too much. I know.
'Who saw in death love's dark immaculate flower.'
They don't warm slippers. Painted houses. Grass.
I don't know where I'm going. Frothy water.
The sound of pouring coal and barking spaniels.
'*Et sur vos lèvres meurent les Caratines.*'

Cows sitting down.
White sugar.
Being in love.
And when one starling leaves,
they all fall over.
The road, the frost, the pram, the spinning spokes.
Two sumptuous new creations drench my body.
Headmistresses adjust their iron gates.
Tearing out the bits about themselves.
The tired Indian waiters slip in snow.
"She calls my girlfriends 'lodgers'."
Concubines!
Words like cats.
Compulsion to repeat.
I smell delicious.
Swimming. Feel my skin.
It is confined to small remoter pools.
'Artists lie most when they tell the truth.'
'A way of life commensurate with their beauty.'
'*Sie lebten mit ihrer Mutter in einer Sandgrube.*'

She was actually giving away the man she loved.
The letter had been opened. Full of pictures.
The road was blocked. They told us to use ladders
specially painted for us by the nurses.
We had to walk through lighted farm buildings.
I don't mean any harm.
My eyes are open.

The bus-conductor says I'm looking kinky.
The poet is God's spy, his velvet cushion.
'...and if not Love, then a very strong desire
to see you RIGHT HERE NOW!'

Cake, golden syrup.
Shouting at the pool.
Don't try to come.
Music pursuing something.
Breaking glass.
Hope D. won't try to come.
It's all gone wrong.
His apartment, his trousers, his books,
his nutmeg smell.

She says why don't I ever brush my hair.

One of my most likely days. Hot weather.
DOMINI EST TERRA 24
Being pregnant makes me feel dishonest.
Now I sleep with foreign men in dreams.
My hand froze on her neck, the dancer said.
Sigmund Freud, I know you can see my knickers.

Long hot babies sleep in ticking taxis.
Compulsive rhyming.
Please don't start again.
Talking in bed. The tranquil bay. The ponies.
Her pale breasts like fish. "No, she's not here."
Pulverous or ductile; not metallic.
Totality of perfect rest.
Afraid.

Ginger ale, paddling, menstruation.
No one but my foe to be my guide.
Hampstead in the autumn, lost for ever.
Wash face, clap hands, cut paper, telephone.
Lie around, read letters, think of sex.
It's snowing and she's cut her perfect hair.
And feared his hopes and hers and all were perished.
He thought about me when I was away.
Virginity – a hive of honey bees.
Four-minute warning.
Pleats.

His sticky fingers.
The blankets are our summer. '...*As ful ofté*

63

Next the foulé netlé, rough and thikké,
The rose waxeth souté and smothé and softé...'

The little ring, the little ruthless lover
who let himself in through the rosy door.
Being good in bed.
Lost by the river.
'Attach yourself to beings, not ideas.'
Hens engender warm simple relationships.
"Your hair-style – what do you call it?"
Mystic grace.

'All your hopes are substitutes for sorrow.'
Distant mountain animals lie dead.
D. is ringing soon. What did I feel like?
He ate his soup in silence like a barge.
Sitting on the steps of the Corn Exchange,
their handbags on their knees.
I think I'm bleeding.

Both the cats are miaowing. We won't feed them.
We think it's much more fun than being kind.
A man in a suit is waving from a sports car.
If only my hair was straight.
The sun is blind.

Exaggeration of physical contact in public.
But what is the point of saving time? she said.
Training a flea. 'Nehru is dead.' Eternity.
"You know your mother thinks you're very ill."
Daddy-long-legs, alder flies, small wasps;
the undulating membrane; we inhale.
Mogadon-entranced, the loving comes.
Chi-chi adores collapsing. Shut the door.

Night positions not so bad. The field.
So this is what it's like!
Our being grounded.
I'm going to be so calm. Christ. Tell the doctor.
I'll catalogue it truly if I do.
Address is very long. What shall I wear?
The grey-green twilight infiltrates my hair.
O Mother, O Mother, provider of comfortable jerseys,
I feel the cold night air ascend the lawn.

CHAPTER 2 **Sons**

Eight babies have been brutally attacked.
The day I saw the nurse, her cheek was bleeding.
His hair was very dark when he was born.
Orange tulips polished by the midwife.
It's silly to be frightened. Look, it's cosy.
He wore his little bonnet which I hated.
She knows when they are crying 'for attention'.
I thought I loved him more than all the rest.

She comes indoors and tidies up his toys.
She puts his cockatoo beside his chair.
She plays him music while he's in his bath.
She told me not to leave him, but I did.
I am the Mother from the Baby Ward.
He's screaming for the breast from which he's torn.

Trixie loves sweet tea.
She rides big horses.
She thinks the ballet dancer's really nice.
The circulating phosphorescent nurses,
stubbing out her endless cigarettes,
whisper things I promise not to tell her.
Trixie darling, rolled in wincyette.

When her daughter left, she kissed the window.
Mary, Mary, go to Intensive Care.
Women walk in different ways with baskets.
One of them's my mother. *Please don't laugh.*
Freshly washed, injected by the nurses,
I fold my lemon candlewick. Goodbye.
She waited for me patiently in VISITORS.
Seven years they said she waited there.

My breasts are rocks of milk.
They found the razor.
The orange flowers kicked the jug again.
Repeated fish are cruising round the curtains.
The giraffes are really nuns.
"She's so fucked-up!"

There's the rabbit, there's the coat I knitted him.
My breasts hang down and brush his lips like pears.
The Sister says I don't look like a mother.
Every day I hear his little prayers.

Little cubes of bread and peanut-butter.
He keeps on falling off the bed.
Don't cry.
The tiny boy the nurse is wheeling in
was seven inches long when he was born.
He's lying underneath his yellow teddy;
he never lets it go; he never smiles.

We like it here. It's cool. I stroke my nightie.
We're going to eat our ices at the zoo.
My socks are blood-soaked but it doesn't matter.
The night nurse is a little baby too.

The babies smell of custard tarts.
Deep breathing.
The after-coming head.
Collapsing wives.
The nurse came in to make my bed. She's knackered!
Milk and blood will cloud the tepid bath.
Fluffy babies make their mothers love them,
fast asleep with prune-juice in their hair.

The gorilla's house is dark.
He wants his biscuits.
He seems to hover on the verge of tears.
We never feel cold.
We are The Mothers.
Found at last, our babies on her knee.

I told him not to hit her but he did.
Who is that little boat for?
Not for me.
Beetroot. Boiled egg. A bowl of custard.
Elephants.
THE SEA OF GALILEE.

I stopped the car, and saw it was a baby.
At first I thought it was a little dog.
I wrapped it in a coat and brought it over.
"He ought to be much quieter, oughtn't he?"

The children are asleep like little bags,
the tulips are as sweet as marzipan,
the cabbages are blue,
the house-boat's red.
The shaggy dog, once so devoted, 's dead.

The sound of heavy boots on the gravel.
It would have been unbearable, I know.
Smoking rollies on the day-room roof-top.
"The first thing that she did was bite the nurse."
I must assume a normal public face.
"She's been here since July."
My eyelids close.
Once D. came in and saw the new day breaking.

My uterus is like a sunlit knife.
He's got a nice big face, I don't know why.
He doesn't smell like us, but of potatoes.

He's like a plum fished out of milky custard.
Endless cries of birds.
The sound of hoeing.

Whenever a child is born, a woman is wasted.
We do not quite belong to ourselves.
Crushing all the hollyhocks with teddies,
the wa-wa babies stumble: "Lift me up!"

You see, it is so lonely I get serious.
Dream of a dream and shadow of a shade.
'The writer's instinct is essentially heartless.'
The wa-wa babies burst into floods of tears.

Cherry nougat for the *quiet* children.
Fond memories –
milk jelly,
sunny weather.
It's far away, and we don't notice it,
or if we do, we don't tell anyone.

We run away and live on bread and chocolate
hidden in the bottom of our prams.

Miles away from anywhere,
like fish.
I want to see a doctor.
I'm in bed.
The boy is tired but happy in the moonlight.
I saw some, falling faster, stuck with blood.
I sleep curled up like shrimps in the darkness.
I long for scenes where man has never trod.
A less soft but a straighter whiteness rises.
Mother Water, I'm your baby now.
A bedside light emits a stream of questions.
Do not console me. I am not your friend.
The yellow flip-flap of the alhatross.
Now snow is filling up my little head.

Like a butcher, deep in rubber buckets,
tearing the hearts from cows' defrosting blood.
Stuck in one position like a statue.
You never lift a finger.
Sunlit bone.
Illuminated gloves. They killed my kitten.
He was the shyest man I ever met.
I wish I was a nice friendly person.
I wonder why he's dirty.
Let's go home.

My father used to sleep in the stables.
My mother knew at once when I made love.
The man who is a bird smokes No. 6's.
"Put your empty packet in the bin."
The nipples floating in the soup are carrots.
My father's got a hornet on his chin.

Far out, the lonely golfers start to cry.

The anorexic suffocates in chocolate.
My father wears a woolly cardigan
with lozenges of fear inside the pocket.

Seafarers gently drift across the ocean
with dogs and chickens in their long canoes
and colonise the islands east of China.

He said it was his wedding. It's not true.

I thought you'd be so pleased –
I shot the rabbits!
Strips of striped pyjamas soaked in tea.
The bulldog's blood drips on the red linoleum.
Her fingernails jump about like fleas.
I think they are thinking of Anna,
washing cherries.
He thought he was a goose.
I'm not surprised!
The driver's going so fast they'll all get flattened.
Beaded whisks of tails to swat fat flies.

Lying on the kitchen floor to hug him.
The doctor should be here any minute.
The yellow parrot saying *What a pity*.
Now his watch is ticking in my ear.
It's true he was my lover. *What a pity*.
The sun needs hearts of warm blood every day.
We're old enough to sleep here in fine weather.
Gertrude Bell has linen-covered thighs.
Jealous of the hands that touched the breasts
he was the first to marvel at. *Don't worry*.
So easily you'd think he's used to it.
The light that fills the world sleeps in my bed.
Waking up from dreams of frozen valleys
and violet bluebells nodding by the pools.
The face of God the doctor said I touched.
And loneliness in pink kneels down to pray.
The bedrooms house a family of camels.
"I hate to see a coffee getting cold."

The doctors say I read too much.
They're staring.
Her mouth is stuffed with custard-yellow wool.

He always hates the girls that he has slept with.
The Psychiatric Unit white with snow.
The red-haired nurse spent all day in the day-room
although she was off-duty.
How do you know?
Enormous jerseys and no knickers. Sand.
Crystallised rose-petals. Ashes. Sheep.
We watched the moorhens treading through the tree-tops,
their big green feet like camels'.
Itchy skin.

Is she quiet and listless all the time,
or is there something I should do, she wondered.
Sitting looking utterly defeated,
fingering the books she's not allowed.
The bullfinches, the bats, the precious letters
gobbled up for nothing.
Go away.

The same good-looking man who liked my cardigan.
Or is that just my illness?
Fairy cakes.
The shaggy remains of a star give sweet instruction
to sleepless lovers.
"What does he mean – he's '*going*'?"
I want to scream and scream and all I do
is write *I want to scream* down in my book.
Fathers coming closer like the tide.
One word.
Enclosed by hate.
I feel like string.
Apricots. Gold. Massed ascensions. Jam.
They're coming now. They're going to flood my veins.

The patients rise like early morning milk.
The planets' movements alternate the tides.
The waiting-room. It frightens me. The hole.
DISEASES OF THE MIND. Pet monkeys. Silk.

Wild bees know little joy.
No visitors.
I've wanted to go home all my life.
Moving deeper into purple woodland.
Lop-eared rabbits, walnuts. Wearing boots.
Ginger weasels cross the gated road.
The little dog is limping.
So am I.
My mother says I'm hopeless.
Bits of lettuce.
The doctor wrote it down:
'Her haunted mind.'

He buttoned up the collar of my jacket
and whispered in my ear 'She's dying now.'
Boiled ham and tulips.
It was evening.
I never want to help you.
"Say Goodbye."

"I like the way you're breathless – it's erotic."
PEOPLE WHO LEAVE LONDON WILL BE SHOT.
Antibiotics. Sleet. My 'fortitude'.
That blissful state in which you feel forgotten.
To get a little carpet in our bedroom,
to go under the door, a little planed.
Afternoons of fruit and acts of kindness.
"Is it true you're not allowed a mirror?"
Your mother called and said she left your washing
crying on the disinfected floor.
A lovely lady's holding out a rabbit.
The lady smiles. The rabbit's name is Pam.
My skirt is like a lorry full of whiskers.
It makes me feel sick to think of him.
The nurse has got a rabbit. Yes, it's mine!
I love its gleaming harmony!
Apologies,
I *used* to have a rabbit I called Pam.

Voices I keep catching all the time.
A mohair cardigan. A bowl of pears.
I know she said don't listen to the voices.
I've been depressed for over twenty years.

All the baby's family are missing.
Espadrilles. Potatoes. Women saints.
Her carrycot is floating in the sea.
It's 4 o'clock. The rabbit's wide awake.
"People say it's all so free and honest."
The walls are green. "He said, 'You're schizophrenic!'"
The feeling of the nurses' hands. I'm blind.
No time for sorrow's rippling fish. I'm blood-soaked.
The corner of the day-room shines like coal.
Soon I will be better. At the moment
I live in humble darkness like the mole.

The gravel drive makes everybody stumble.
The Virgin in her wooden dress is kind.
Red roses tumble softly onto water.
The day-room smells of toffee. I don't mind.

"Loving me is not enough." He laughed,
feeling with his fingers up my skirt.
He looked into my frightened, rubber eye-balls.
He smelt of fennel, weasels, sandy dirt.

Inmates waltz at dusk at party-time.
Sitting by herself in fairyland.
"It's far too late to start remembering now!"
The smell of fennel when they move. Thick tea.
The sun is setting. It is time to start.
"Everyone admires our Christmas Tree!"

Sausages and chips and apple crumble.
Everything she does is always wrong.
The vicar gave us lovely cards and honey.
The rich girl says her father won't be long.

Fluffy hands and horses fill the sky.
I do not need a coat. *Leave me alone.*
The red-eyed doctors block the corridors
with turquoise needles tipped with Methadone.

The rocks like leopards soften in the rain.
I see myself as Jesus' private nun,
lost in the mists of time, when we were little –
mushrooms; herons; woolly bears; my mum.

I had to cross the day-room on my hands,
a silent rabbit foraging for fruit.
I dread the human voice. The doctor said
"There's nothing we can do. We need your bed."

The daily wards of underwater fame.
Swimming to the pills.
Don't say my name.

The hospital is underwater, Trixie.
To widen brains, please nail all joints loosely.

This little thing's been homeless for so long
Now say goodbye.
She won't be very long.

PART TWO

The Out-Patient

I step across the white dust of the runway
towards a man with pistols for a face.
He's tall and thin with one hand in a bandage.
I hear a faint *pow-pow* of disgrace.

'Departing for womanhood.' Crap. Green velvet cushions.
The baker's sons are being introduced.
The canteen of the airport smells of pepper.
I follow him towards the setting sun.
The avenue of cacti like an elephant
shelter silent groups of staring men.
We go upstairs. His buckle scrapes the brick-work.
Lust and grief. Unusual cakes. He's kind.
I'm menstruating on a stranger's blankets.
Sorrow like a silver spool unwinds.

The sun is hot. My head is full of silence
attracting hordes of angry bees like bells.
A swallow-tail, an amber necklace, henna.
I want to be so calm. 'Devotion frees.'

People, horizontal, lit, ascending,
now declare their everlasting love
by open windows, where the tepid evening
is tempting them to cast aside their clothes.

See me see me see me in the garden.
I'm made of ants.
Whose voice is that?
It's hers.
Feel between my legs two lips like lollies,
or like a blood-hound on the verge of tears.

Talking to him in a voice as distant
as unborn daughters kneeling by my bed.

Turkish delight, brazil nuts, sweetened yoghourt.
I treasure every word I think he said.

The only men were doctors. We were dollies
put to sleep in resonating halls.

The bell is ringing like an English cherry.
Picasso in his villa touches girls.

74

The boots that crush the roses hear me whisper
You mustn't kiss me now. He takes my hand.
Ecstasy, which makes him feel nearer,
has made me ill. I never talk. I'm banned.

The offices are empty, only you:
a violet light, a pleated skirt, a prayer
rising in the dark then drifting downward
to join the other voices of the air;
while in the muted villa, calmed by sorrow,
someone feels a lightening of snow.
We'll move you to another bed tomorrow,
we'll move you to a place where good girls go.

Bluebells, Bovril, somebody's blind spaniel.
The bluebells shine with Daddy's violet light.

She even brought her mole with her. *Don't cry.*
She ran about the rocks till it was night.

Toast and cream. Her deep-blue velvet dresses.
I haven't told the others where I've been.

Dragonflies fly round her head in traces.
There may be someone there – we'll have to see.

Someone to talk to, cold as charity.
An analgesic and a febrifuge.

Lop-eared sheep in echoing ravines.
The tiny nun is venturing to intrude.

Lamented daughters slip away like cats;
running water; seals; grace abounding:

a crippled Coptic mother's early sorrows,
through centuries of beaten earth resounding.

The doctors say my shyness is repellent.
The shyness of the bittern. I'm alone,

living in a world where pinks and pumas
drink cherry-flavoured drops of Methadone.

The other people cut down all the trees
and vivisect the cats and toads. *Roulette.*

Making honey sandwiches. Misgivings.
The way my mother handles ducks. *Nanette.*

Even the Central Predigstuhl's West Gully
denied us shelter in its icy palace.

Irish monks in frail craft made of leather
discovered Iceland, glaciers and solace.

The golden dribbles of the butterscotch
tremble on the rubber. She can't swim.

She's singing like a lover through the water,
singing through the glass her blue-green hymn.

Crystal quartz like love from Colorado.
Sealed with rheum. The chickens' sunlit meal

scattered on the lily-pond. '*Raw, tender,*
hostile, hot or bored – how do you feel?'

I feel like a table-cloth with grazing rights;
a newt; a guinea-fowl; a tulip-head;

the listlessness of rivers' eels; bandages.
Don't tell me what you think I should have said!

My body's like a zebra's; rock-hard plums;
the glittering of quartz washed by the sea;

Dorothy Wordsworth's toothache, like a crystal;
TEACH YOURSELF KARATE; amber tea.

Measuring my sleeping lover's neck.
Chicken thighs. A greeting. *Take your time.*

Running water soothes; a little music.
I can't imagine what it's like. *Like mine.*

His hand is lying on my lap like liver.
Wiping up the blood. He's very kind.

Every little star must twinkle brighter.
The poor thing's got no breasts. *O never mind.*

Bunches of butchered seagulls. Dusky archers.
You must be someone special. *Hold my hand.*

Bit by bit, not suddenly. Peach. Barley.
I thought you were never coming. *Hold my hand.*

The handsome sleeping generals lie massacred
like beautiful white flour from Singapore.

Who but a beaten specialist would offer
to map the changes of the ocean floor?

I didn't say a word about the therapy.
The doctors deal in glitter-coated worms.

A schizophrenic dressed in silk to please him,
I part my lips like lilac, brush his sperm.

I think the nurse said she was going to shoot me.
I can't sit up. I don't know what to say.

The bead-like packing may be tiny pearls. *Hush*,
everyone loves fear. Don't go away.

The shaved and beaded Maasai mothers calmly
wash their sons in milk from special cows.

He said that if I walk along serenely,
I'm worthy of their gold and violet flowers.

They broke into my room, and I was murdered –
innocent, illuminated, rose.

I cannot touch my cup in case they see me.
My mother leaves my laundry with the nurse.

She turns the light out, leaving me in darkness,
a dumb, adored, impassive amulet:

ah, I will be so lovely in the summertime,
when Doctor parts my sleepy body's net.

The central point round which the volumes settle,
his doll is staring like the smell of gas.

He wants to be alone with me. I'm sweating.
My body will dissolve. "Can't you relax?"

Sunny days of quiet desperation.
"She misses her poor daughter still, you know!"

Sunlight. Netball. Ankle-socks. White rabbits.
Ceaseless prayer like purity of snow.

Rescued from her introverted nightmare
by seeing washing billowing on the line.

Doing certain things. "Yes, please sit anywhere!"
We sit on any surface we can find.

'Write a list of gratifying activities.'
Tomato juice makes glasses hard to clean.

Suddenly the man leans down and bites me.
The lily-pond – the carp – the bluebells' gleam.

The gods of Europe shower me with smiles,
unnerving all the men that come and stare;

I dance until my heart begins to break –
then Sister comes and makes me brush my hair.

The dog has got a little curly tail
the size and texture of a tangerine.

The bluebells are as glossy as the horses,
galloping like lust into the sea.

The penned imported camels by the villa,
like ghostly castles made of sand and bone,

lean their narrow hips against the darkness,
waiting for a love they've never known.

I am alone. Where are they? Snowy weather.
Am I allowed to write like this or not?
She said that I could go to the meeting,
and then she said that I had better not.

The girl in my room is reading ALONE WITH OTHERS.
I really feel I can't go through with this.
'Walking through a forest with a parcel.'
And all she wants is my companionship.

Chicory, cashew nuts, paper zebras.
"Why do you look so worried?" I don't know.
The voices fade. The floor is piled with cushions.
I wonder, will she speak when we're alone?

We are the children of This. This is the silence.
I haven't talked to anyone for years.
I can hear a pony's rhythmic cropping.
I can feel the wind against my ears.

"It's been a lovely friendly convalescence,
and I shall go home feeling much much better…"
It's miles getting back…but we don't care…
miles and miles…it really doesn't matter.

Larches in the forest bring the evening.
Disabled men drink milk among fat hens.
A sense of loss like violins pursues me
and will not let me sleep, the young man says.

Piano Pieces, fruit, embroidered slippers.
Struggle for what? Eurhythmy. Green and neat,
scentless mayweed, dragonflies, tall grasses
ripple in the grounds like greyhounds' feet.

The man who dances like the sea surrounds me.
I'm shivering. I'm sorry. It's so new.
The Spiritual Head of the Order's started laughing.
Piles of strawberry jam. "May I laugh too?"

As blossom fills the lawns of scented gardens,
fluttering whispers fill the patient's throat.
Love is more than simple acts of kindness:
it comes from deep within us like a note.

They play the flute until it's nearly morning.
The man who heals with sound is by my side.
My meditation's swilled with icy water
for Ahto and Vellamo, Ahto's bride.

Horses pass unseen in the forest,
a speckled bantam suddenly takes flight;
Molly, who is over eighty, 's mending
the wooden boat she painted gold last night.

"What does he mean by meditation anyway?"
She looks so lonely with her little plaits.
Secret letters. Failing to adore him.
Invisible vanilla. Roses. Cats.

The dogs are neither elegant nor handsome,
but make us feel warm when we are cold.
The sleeping monks are sailing into morning;
soya milk like cowries; silence; gold.

Tinned faces. Yellow cushions. *Love him more.*
And let your body say what you can't say.
It's just a little shower, she said, her suffering.
It's nice to know you like me. "It's OK"

She said that I could join the group tomorrow –
her tilted pools of everlasting wealth!
Someone in my dream is always smiling.
'You think it must be God but it's yourself.'

Community of nuns in Andalusia.
Colossal love like thunder. Bowls of shells.
The dancer had a giant dog called Hilda
who used to like to eat the daffodils.

The patient from the villa came to visit.
Rabbit fur, damp leaves. She didn't stay.
The Sister has retired to the country –
irises and blackbirds, flowering may.

Like mottled soap of olive-oil and soda;
Nivea; flat stones, their edges gone;
the soles of people paddling in the tide-line,
I feel I am being acted on.

Gardening gloves touch pale blue hydrangeas;
'becoming aware of myself as something known';
my dog has gone to sleep across my pillow;
keep the mind in the middle of the tongue.

The hooded men who follow me and whisper
have slipped away like weasels in the snow.
I too must say good-bye to the monastery.
The train is waiting. "Really, I must go!"

PART THREE

The Last Week

Friday

And all the time,
the heifers' solemn faces
are breathing by my side,
as soft as ash;
my little fire
is burning in the moonlight
that slips between the grasses
like a cat.

Saturday

The painted bows.
The silver nail-scissors.
Strips of paper in a stencilled tin.
A flannel in a bowl.
Hush. What's the matter?
Early morning sunlight, paper-thin.

My breath is like the long electric hair
of someone swinging on a high trapeze:
it sweeps the air and all the faces cry
ha; and again *ha!*
WHAT TURNS YOU ON?

Sunday

The river-bank is thick with summer flowers,
as stiff as pigs, as pink as fruit; massed flies
stroke their wings against the fluted sky
whose height, as sweet as hay, rings like an axe
and dyes the spotted cows a million blues.

Monday

At midnight we have rolls and oranges.
My hands are cold.
They make me cups of tea.
Sons and daughters, singing in the moonlight,
are drifting on their tin beds out to sea.

Ankle-bones,
peach-slices,
mignonette;
bars of chocolate,
fur:
I won't forget.

Tuesday

I'm sitting on my blanket
eating toast.
In India I starved.
I'm very fat.
Mother Teresa, Mother Teresa calling.
She wants me now.
She wants me in her flat.

Wednesday

A lame man walks for miles along a beach;
the dazzling sunlight magnifies his dreams:
a pool of blood that soaks into the pine-woods,
a bungalow, dead rabbits, skin-tight jeans.

Thursday

The afternoon
is giving way
to evening,
I help my tearful daughter
rinse her hair;
a bullfinch
in the holm oak
calmly singing;
my holiday;
Nijinsky;
ginger air.

My sleeping-bag smells sweetly
of the pine-wood,
my smoky hair and pillows
of warm stones.
The terns fly off like splinters of the evening.
I'm glad there's no one here.
Peach-slices.
Bones.

Friday

My sister has been racing someone's race-horse
across a valley in the pouring rain,
trying to forgive
our blood-stained mother
who killed her German Shepherd,
Violet.

The Minuet for Berenice is playing;
everything seems normal, but it's not:
we look as if we're drawing, but we're praying;
our studio of birds, our brotherhood.

Instant mashed potato, lettuce, Spam.
The rabbit on the plate is going shopping.
The islands of potato warm the lettuce
and stir the little virgin jockey's heart.

The Boyle Family. Walsingham. Hot water.
"She hasn't left her drawing-board all day."
The warm dog and the Little Tern run quietly
to Everlasting Light on pointed toes.

Saturday

Your voice is clear as crystal,
so is mine;
as turquoise,
divers,
steel,
turpentine.
Your fingers smell of Nivea,
it's cold,
your fingers smell of pine-woods and the sky;
you touch my hands,
you wash my eyes in water
enclosed in heated towels. *Say goodbye.*

'Every sort of pine will yield resin
for incense, violins and ballet-shoes.
The creamy tears are found in natural fissures,
or trickling from the wounds of broken boughs.'

The boats are on the grass,
the sun is shining,
the station-master tends his flower-bed.
I feel I am dancing underwater
and Christ is by my side, the dancer said.

A LITTLE BOOK OF MEAT
(1993)

'If you need to ask, you'll never know'

REGINA CLINE O'CONNOR
to her daughter Flannery O'Connor

Lust

Lust's the answer – lust
like pessaries
that glide along my veins;
like gilded lozenges.

Beyond the dunes,
where soldiers eat soft chocolate,
palaces are falling.
Lust's the answer.

Little Sisters

Up to their angelic necks in steers and guinea fowl,
there are girls growing up into women
without knowing why;
there are duck-feeding mothers
and duck-feeding, stern-faced daughters,
their dresses smelling of church
and giant azaleas,
who haven't the slightest idea
what they've got coming to them;
who toil away,
gingerbread-mixing,
geranium-nursing,
fancy-breed-raising,
permanent-waving,
inspired by the jelly-eating Sisters of St Joseph of Corondolet,
by the Little Sisters of the Poor, whom no one knows,
by little angels –
daughters who think they understand everything,
who practise fudge- and crystallized-violet-giving,
who breed glum swans,
and wobbly spotted mules,
for whom the only males are bulls and cobs,
and the only man they know is the Man they don't,
Who might appear out of the woods at any moment,
with blood on His hands like a sunset,
and somehow redeem them;
whose private lives are disturbed
by the sound of a van
with somebody nobody's asked for, or wants, at the wheel.

Auction Day

While I was quietly doing nothing all day
but feeding the geese their stale corn-kernels
and manicuring the Guernseys
in preparation for the Registered-Guernsey-Cow Auction-Day,
something irresistible
lurched into my life,
something unknown, from nowhere, with eyes like Alaska,
and growls,
and sighs,
and offers of what it proclaims will be Permanent Joy
in exchange for a home,
in exchange for a home with me.
So what am I supposed to do, Our Lady
– casserole it?
What am I supposed to do I want to know.

Our Lady of Meat

Our Lady of Meat,
Our Lady of goose,
Our Lady of pain;
Our Lady of lips,
Our Lady of nipples,
Our Lady of jelly;
Our Lady of house-coats,
Our Lady of wedding-dresses,
Our Lady of sweet peas;
Our Lady of Calomel,
Our Lady of vans,
Our Lady of jam;
Our Lady of casseroles,
Our Lady of corn-kernels,
Our Lady of Virginity, and Renunciation, and resisting things;
Our Lady of nothing,
Our Lady of never,
Our Lady of Love –
what am I supposed to do I'd like to know?

Don't Let's Talk About Being in Love

Don't let's talk about being in love, OK?
– about *me* being in love, in fact, OK?
about your bloated face, like a magnolia;
about marsupials,
whose little blunted pouches
I'd like to crawl inside, lips first;
about the crashing of a million waterfalls
– as if LOVE were a dome of glass beneath a lake
entered through a maze of dripping tunnels
I hoped and prayed I'd never be found inside.

At night I dream that your bedroom's crammed with ducks.
You smell of mashed-up meal and scrambled egg.
Some of the ducks are broody, and won't stand up.
And I dream of the fingers of your various wives
reaching into your private parts like beaks.
And you're lying across the bed like a man shouldn't be.
And I'm startled awake by the sound of creaking glass
as if the whole affair's about to collapse
and water come pouring in with a rush of fishes
going *slurpetty-slurpetty-slurp* with their low-slung mouths.

The Devastation of Easter Island

I don't know if you've ever
waited for someone to smile at you,
but if you have, you'll know how I'm feeling now:
all the other smiles for all the other people
fall and melt
like snow from another age
forming rivers where beautiful women are walking
down avenues of trees into the sea;
but all I want
is for *you* to smile at *me*.

I don't know if you've ever
wanted someone to stretch out their hand and touch you,
someone who's been sitting beside you all afternoon
like an uninhabited stone
and driving you mad;
or like a ceremonial stone fish-hook
you're desperate, you're praying, to be fished by –
but if you have,
you'll know how I'm feeling now.

You're numb as hair,
as mute as cats,
as soft as lettuces,
as resolute and mysterious
as the cause of the devastation of Easter Island
where nothing remains except heads,
and a few long-legged chickens
that don't mind drinking sea-water.

I don't know if you've ever
done nothing all day but *languish*,
but if you have, you'll know how I'm feeling now.

Sleepless Nights

Because you scream like a sluice,
because you scream like someone waking up at night
with raging toothache,
like a cargo of half-wrapped lorries
being unloaded into some remote terminal
with lots of shouting and gesticulation;
like the Mongolian Empire itself,
thundering with obese horesemen;
because the last night I spent longing for you
was like spending the night with no clothes on
in a Daimler full of chows
with the windows closed,
I have decided to calm myself down,
and imagine my head as a tinkly moss-padded cavern
where nothing happens.

Ignore Me

Ignore me.
I went to sleep last night quite normally,
but in the morning I was someone else, not me –
someone who's been wallowing in dreams of you
like pea-hens in a stranger's flower-beds;
who's heavy with desire
like sacks of meat;

who gets to her feet, crashes about
like a two-legged escaped rhinoceros
in pursuit of anyone who looks remotely,
or sounds remotely, or smells remotely,
like you – then mumbles forlornly *I'm sorry*.
I'm sorry.
Ignore me.

I Think About You All the Time

I think about you all the time. I think:
that you live in a world of meals cooked by cooks;

that someone like me's quite wrong for someone like you;
that I owe my energy to the squashed pituitary glands

of thousands of little pigs butchered daily
at the Armour Packing Plant in Chicago, Illinois.

And in my dreams you're giving me Chicago.
And in my dreams I'm resurrecting pigs.

North Carolina

Everything about you's a bit like me –
in the same way that North Carolina's a bit like Ribena
but rhymes with Vagina, which is nearly the same,
but much darker –
brutal and sweet like disease,
sweet as an asphalt dealer.

Imagine a cloud.
Imagine eating a cloud.
Imagine your mouth being full of the cloud like the world.
And imagine a person like me with a person like you.
I have turned you into a cloud.
Prepare to be eaten.

The Longing of the Meat Trade

The longing of the meat trade
for dead pets,

of icy waters
for the lost Titanic;

the longing of a stadium
for heroes

is like a whim
compared to mine for you.

Speak To Me

I'm going to stop.
I'm going to start again.
I'm going to make strategic little piles
of things like cigarettes and sugar-cubes,
and bantams' eggs, and cubes of cattle-cake,
and range them, along your route,

until you notice them;
and then I'm going to balance
slightly larger things,
like fish, or fruit, or tulips, on my head,
whispering as I walk: *Speak to me*;
whispering *Speak to me please.*

I Have Never Been to Africa

I have never been to Africa –
I've only seen it in my dreams
and longed to go there –
it looked like a giant peach, half-asleep,
gracefully draped in a dried civet-cat skin
someone had sewn small bells and teeth across,
and dancing figures made of ivory
that carry miniature gongs
and miniature hoes –

so no, I've never been to Africa,
and now I just find it embarrassing
to remember sitting in your van
reading MAIN BEAM MAIN BEAM
over and over again, or not even reading it,
but sitting in front of it,
imagining bream, and roach,
flapping lugubriously around our ears
as the van fills up with water;

to remember sitting in your van
trying to impress you
with stories of my travels
that couldn't possibly have been true,
and the van piled high with boxes of shopping,
of hats and coats,
of slinky satin shirts;
boxes of ants
to feed the googling bream.

What the Night Was Made For

Can a very small grandmother,
alone in a room with a pigeon,
learn to fly?

Can a very small grandmother,
even one accustomed to tinkering
with second-hand tractors,
carve up a large man at a wall sink
with the swiftly-rotating discs
of a cement-cutter,
and stow him in eighteen plastic rubbish sacks,
and leave no blood?

And can a very small grandmother
follow the goats around the disused aerodrome,
because she is learning to draw,
and likes their minty eyes and angularity,
without arousing suspicion?

And can a little nun-like daughter like me
be left alone
with a blood-spattered man like you?

And can you tell me
what the night was made for?

Leaving Mother

What do you think I think about, I wonder?
Do you think I think I wish I was your lover?
And what do you think when you think I think like that?

Do you think I think I'd leave the farm and Mother
and hens and cows and woods to live with you?
Or do you think, like me, you must not think?

Think about nothing but nothing,
nothing but *No*, nothing for miles and miles
but *No* on *No*?

My Senior Peacock

My senior peacock with his wall-eyed eyeball's
not so stubborn and superior as you –

why don't you do the not-done thing occasionally,
and encourage *me*
to do the not-done thing you want to do wrong, too?

Such as?
Such as we could go off together somewhere,
just the two of us,
and I could sew you a special sleeper-suit,
and train you to walk backwards
like my bantam;

and we could go out somewhere;
and you wouldn't have to be so serious
and high-minded all the time.
And we could be friends
and talk to one another.

And I wouldn't mind a certain inexperience.
And you wouldn't mind disintegrating hips.

Tomatoes

When I am woken up
by somebody else's lover's
comatose leg on my arm,
cold on the pillow beside me
like a discarded trepanning instrument –

when I am woken up
by a whole string of adjectives
describing my beautiful face –

when I am woken up
by awkward vibrations
disturbing the sweet Georgia air;
by the chandelier starting to drop,
and the balcony collapsing
as I limp out –

when I am woken up
by a lover, or someone dressed as a lover,
elaborately describing their dream –

when my sentences,
instead of flying off like swallows
to distant countries,
lie tangled like spillikins
under the dark hood
of her loved one's plum-coloured eiderdown –

I am about to be made love to
for the first time;
I am about to be crushed
like a bagful of dusty biscuits
under a rolling-pin.

I will get up,
remove a bar of chocolate
from its pile at the back of the fridge,
and walk out into the deserted yard.

I will not notice
the mat of jewels,
the finches,
nor the pleas
that rattle on my head like pure hail.

All I will see is cement,
and the dreamer's placid zebras
having tomatoes hurled against their stripes.

All I will hear is the zoo,
and zoo noises:
caged animals' unseemly
scratches and grunts.

Cattle

I live in a world of bulls and yellow fruit.
I live in a world of sturdy bulls on chains
whose herds of swaying cows are my companions,
their lips and tails and teats
all drooling and warm.

But my obsession with you –
like a speeding car with a knocking exhaust pipe
driven downhill by a party of Whirling Dervishes
with faces like lonely motels –
has upset them.
My obsession –
which goes down on fifty thousand bended knees
and prays for me, like the world's longest monk –
has upset them.

The sponge-cake and the one-eyed swan,
the bell for mass,
the tractor man,
this curious electric typewriter,
soft fruit and yellow flowers,
have been upset:
I live in a world of cows insane with longing.
Mother has made us a pond we can lie down in.

For Days Now I Have Been Imagining It

For days now I have been imagining it:
my taking a deep breath,
my stepping into the room,
your coming slowly towards me
as a lily might –
but what will become of us then,
I want to know:
will it be over?

In spite of our secrets,
as rare and painfully inadequate
as the tadpoles of the forested regions of Borneo;

in spite of our faith,
grim as a mountain range
which we climb and climb,
never to reach the summit,
with its unparalleled views of the surrounding countryside;

in spite of the sheets,
in violet, cerise and mint,
that a nocturnal well-wisher left at the door for us,
will it be over?

And if you think I am going to sit here all afternoon
dreaming about our future,
you're absolutely right:
I'm going to pick you up
like a bridegroom made of sugar on a wedding-cake,
with sugar bones,
and carry you off to the bruised lakes of the future –
with bracelets, cinnamon and shampoo,
we will set up home together on the banks,
just us, and a knee-high moon,
and a few yurts.

A Cow Eating Carrots

This ziggurat of putrefying carrots,
the size and shape of an ancient Chevrolet

made of jellied milk and oranges
caramelised on top to make it crunchy,

is how I think of you; I think of me
alternately chewing and drooling, like the cow.

My Italian Cardigan

I owe my Italian cardigan to my cousin;
I owe my new bulb to my aunt;
I owe the death of the black Diamond Rattlesnake
in the shrubbery to Jack;
I owe to a failure of nerve
my well-mannered battery of euphemisms,
which have failed for so long
to call this, this; and that, that; and love, love;
and I owe my sudden, unseemly, quite un-called-for
so-called love,
which is more like You-Know-What,
to You-Know-Who.

Suppose, at the back of an aeroplane,
there was a little balcony
which people could be led to, and sat down on,
and left to themselves in the sky in,
gripping the railings,
to be bumped through the clouds at topspeed
like no one from nowhere to nowhere,
their hearts in their mouths, feeling sick,
but going so fast they can't even go on and *be* sick –
that's like my love,
my feverish love,
for you.

Her Curious Hat

Space is for walking across deserts in,
from dropping into from painted helicopters,
for bleeding in;

space is for sailing ships across,
for listening to,
and being silent in;

space is where tininess goes,
and five thousand years of glass,
and barbecued prawns;

swimming Alsatians,
Van Gogh's baby,
eels;

and Ma,
in her curious silicon rubber hat,
trying to overcome her fear of water.

Where to Fish in Catalonia

If I lie down,
I might feel better;
if I smell the chill
of the almost inaccessible
high-mountain bear-skull sanctuary;
if I feel the silence
of oil poured on oil –

but I just say *speak to me please* –
in a voice as rasping
as a beetle trying vainly to escape
from an increasingly airless jam-jar
embedded in my brain
like a fossilized pistol;
or the silhouettes of jazz-fans
climbing everywhere you look
with huge cases.

If I lie down,
I might feel better.
If I observe the snow,
meet masons,
measure milk;
rub, boil or chip hard seeds
until they germinate;
if I plant forests at will,
I might feel better.
If I study *Where to Fish in Catalonia*,
and dress in silk,
I think I might feel better –

but I never stop inventing
my long intimate conversations with you,
and I never stop missing your van.

If only I were to lie down on the ground
with my head under a blanket
and count fish,
I might feel better,
as they oodle about
in their warm relaxing shoals.

A Small Hotel

My nipples tick
like little bombs of blood.

Someone is walking
in the yard outside.

I don't know why
Our Lord was crucified.

*A really good fuck
makes me feel like custard.*

Los Cocodrilos de Méjico

Of course I know that I'm not a curled-up shrimp
lost in a world of nothing but snow and ice;
that you're not reading *Los Cocodrilos de Méjico*
because you are a large green creature
with yellow teeth that I can't get out of my head,
but because you like using your brain,
and are learning Spanish;
that you are not an electrician;
that you are not a parakeet;
that you do not provide people in wedding-dresses
with buzzes and squawks like simultaneous orgasms or "peaks";
that you are not walking into town
with a pramful of tulips
to lay at my door;
that the water in the bay is blue and tranquil.
Why else would someone walk into the sea?

The Graceful Giraffe of Clot Bey

When I ascend the terrace steps of Potsdam
between the yew trees clipped to look like polyps,
or a colony of polyps, by cold water,
with no one about on the steps except myself,
having no language but this –
I certainly need you.

When I hear the risen storks,
the cries from whose long coiled throats
can't help sounding mournful,
as if entire courts together with their kings
are slain, dismembered and buried
in valleys that now lie barren –
I certainly need you.

When I say goodbye
with the same dejected air
I imagine Giacometti would wear
if, torn from his work
and his beautiful brother Diego,
he was set on the deck of a ship
bound for an island inhabited by nothing but tortoises
lumbering about on volcanoes
like abandoned radiators;

when I wave
like sallow mutants discarding limbs
in twilit marshland settlements
where only the rats survive;

when my eyes blur,
like the graceful giraffe's of Clot Bey
who continued to gladden the hearts of Parisians
for sixteen years before she died,
mute and majestic,
sunk on her bed of straw –
I certainly need you.

When the telephone,
like a bricked-up cathedral,
refuses to ring;
like a one-hundred-fingered ice-encrusted orchestra,
primed,
beribboned,
and triumphant,
which refuses to strike up and play
without its seraphic conductor –
I certainly need you.

Baby clams wilt in yellow brine.
Van Gogh's ear wilts in a jar in a police station.
My heart, equally forsaken,
wilts in the screw-top jar of your not coming.

Coition

You'll have to lie perfectly still
like a nude with a rat;

and when I have finished,
you'll have not a hair on your head,

and everyone else in the world
will have gone to sleep.

Peafowl

Forty desultory peafowl, raised by me,
are posing on my milk-crates,
cupboards,
crutches,
taps
and enemas.

When people die,
one sees them playing croquet,
singing,
weaving:
In my case, I'll be someone one avoids –
being screeched at by, and screeching at, vain peafowl.

What Do I Really Believe?

I believe that Benedictine
tastes like a meteor;

I believe that antitheses and hyperboles
dilate like slowly eaten fruit;

I believe that when a man takes long, deep breaths
he is trying not to prematurely ejaculate;

that tangerines are oranges, and full of juice,
and do not move unless they are being carried;

that the idea of repelling the rabbits
with moth flakes was not a success;

that abbatoirs binge
on Santa Gertrudis bulls;

that if I meet someone I like,
I start to do it unconsciously;

that a prisoner is painting the bars of his cell sky-blue,
and a tall giraffe is living in a summer-house in Maine;

that Beethoven was so deaf
he thought he was a painter;

that giant slugs
can be bigger than chihuahuas;

that I always seem to get
the wrong end of the stick;

that I love you very much,
but it doesn't seem to make the slightest difference;

that it's all very well
but why don't you love me too?

that there ought to be a law against chihuahuas,
that no one has to groom a giant slug.

The Bed

This is the bed
that I became a woman in,
that I lay naked on on tepid nights,
after my grandmother's scaly-fingered gardener
half-marched, half crept in here and mended it
(like a man mends a cage in a zoo,
with excited reluctance);
I lay in the shade
of this lop-sided wardrobe –
that looks like a caramelized ungainly antelope
with nothing between its head and the constellations
except the occasional stiff-winged aeroplane –

and sent my long gold clitoris to sea
between my legs, streamlined and sweet
like a barge
laden with sweetmeats and monkeys
bound for some distant land;
and this is the bed I saw the chickens from,
running across the yard without their heads,
and smelt the farmers
leaning on their cows that had cars' names –
a smell of blood and milking and desire
I was suddenly part of, and sunk in,
like necks in Startena.

Hippos

Glistening hippos float about like chocolate
bumping into everything. They're you.
I don't know what's come over me.
I do. For three days now
I've been on the straight and narrow.
I come indoors. To what?
To thoughts of you: veiled hippopotami,
trying to be invisible, romping
with their eyes closed in my bedroom.

Much Against Everyone's Advice

Much against everyone's advice,
I have decided I must not be put off any longer
from coming into the yard
and telling you the truth, as best I can.
There's something I've got to tell you I will say.
Yes, I have been practising, you see –
you would be proud of me.
Alone in this ridiculous café,
with stiffened hair,
holding your last letter
like a penitent teenager
stranded on a cliff
who clutches the Bible
thank God she remembered to bring,
I have been practising.

Do you remember the boat
that dropped from the sky
right into Granma's garden,
just as two little girls,
never to visit fairyland again,
strayed out of the pecan grove?
And Granma turned over in her sleep
and saw a blond young pilot
who looked like Jesus
gazing into her eyes
from just about the level of her bedroom window?
Who ran his hands backwards and forwards
along his glossy cockpit
as if it were a prize bull
and not a stunted machine
that had ruined our lives forever;
who looked down at the boat
as if she were a dancer, in perfect order,
and not a boat
creaking among squashed roses in our border?

All year he had been practising for this,
and I have too.
Much against everyone's advice,
I have decided to tell you everything
– poor worm.

Cow

I want to be a cow
and not my mother's daughter.
I want to be a cow
and not in love with you.
I want to feel free to feel calm.
I want to be a cow who never knows
the kind of love you 'fall in love with' with;
a queenly cow, with hips as big and sound
as a department store,
a cow the farmer milks on bended knee,
who when she dies will feel dawn
bending over her like lawn to wet her lips.

I want to be a cow,
nothing fancy –
a cargo of grass,
a hammock of soupy milk
whose floating and rocking and dribbling's undisturbed
by the echo of hooves to the city;
of crunching boots;
of suspicious-looking trailers parked on verges;
of unscrupulous restaurant-owners
who stumble, pink-eyed, from stale beds
into a world of lobsters and warm telephones;
of streamlined Japanese freighters
ironing the night,
heavy with sweet desire like bowls of jam.

The Tibetans have 85 words for states of consciousness.
This dozy cow I want to be has none.
She doesn't speak.
She doesn't do housework or worry about her appearance.
She doesn't roam.
Safe in her fleet
of shorn-white-bowl-like friends,
she needs, and loves, and's loved by,
only this –
the farm I want to be a cow on too.

Don't come looking for me.
Don't come walking out into the bright sunlight
looking for me,

black in your gloves and stockings and sleeves
and large hat.
Don't call the tractorman.
Don't call the neighbours.
Don't make a special fruit-cake for when I come home:
I'm not coming home.
I'm going to be a cowman's counted cow.
I'm going to be a cow
and you won't know me.

The Convent of Sleep

If you are a good, calm person,
you join the convent of sleep
and are heard from no more for the rest of the night;
but if you are a worrier and fantasiser,
you roam about the borders of your dream-world
getting into all sorts of trouble,
and drawing the wrath of people
who don't believe in anything that makes sense,
and are full of secrets and irregularities,
down on your head like a hood.

Think of the pain.
Think of the silence.
Think of the silence aboard the Mignonette
after the two crew members killed and ate the cabin boy;
think of their mothers
falling in love with their fathers;
think of the pain of falling in love,
and don't.
Just sleep good clean hard sleeps
like white potatoes rolling down the middle of the night.

This Afternoon I Swallowed a Cornfield

This afternoon I swallowed a cornfield,
and three painted water-towers
and a pecan grove,
and a gravel pit I'd never seen before,
and the warm creamy lake at the bottom of it,
and the panama hat
that was quietly circling around it,
and the little man who suddenly sprang up
and ran away towards a deserted railway station
and stepped into a carriage
without looking back,
but whose face –
in spite of the heat,
in spite of my being half-dizzy
beside where a cornfield was,
in spite of my trying to fail to remember who you are –
whose face,
like a deer that's no more than the thought of a deer,
no more than a wish in the air,
was unquestionably yours.
That's what I do.
I swallow things.
I lie and dream and sweat and swallow things.

I Want to Run Away

I want to run away into the woods;
to kill weasels in wheat silos;
to live in the woods,
with my disfigured face exposed,
without a name;
to stay in the woods
until I belong to the woods –
and if somebody finds me alive,
and they may,
they'll shoot.
Ma will have said she's a liar, and armed,
and to shoot.

I heard of a mother once
who kept her daughter
under the floorboards: *Mother,*
do it to me please. Mother, do it to me.
When I'm not being me being me,
but just being dumb,
she likes it.
And the more half-witted I am,
the more she likes it.
Stuff me under the floorboards. Crack my knees.
And if I am not to your liking,
shoot me please.

Crossing the Desert in a Pram

And when my ears fill up with sand,
and everything goes quiet,

lie down in the hood with me.
Pretend the sand is fur.

They'll find us with a little beeping tube
that finds rare animals. They think I am a shoe.

The leader of the expedition
can't believe his luck.

He waves the shoe about above his head...
Relax, I hear her say, *my dear, relax.*

What Are Fields For?

What are fields for?
To go long-jumping with you and Thomas Merton on.
What is scaffolding for?
To see the tiny buildings below us from.
What are sheets for?
To be wrapped up with you all night in.
And what is this longing for?
And why is it always you I'm thinking of?
I think of you.
Why you?
It's always you.
You're eating tomato ice-cream with a long spoon.
You're copying out the entire Bible by hand,
book by book.
You're dismantling scaffolding.
You're hiking with a mattress in the rain.
You're abandoning a naked baby
on the front steps of an Old People's Home.
You're frying my one-legged pea-chick.
You're at a station.
And I say to myself 'Say *Make yourself numb* to yourself.
Say *Make yourself make yourself numb*.
Say *Take no notice*.
Trample on his arms and legs and universe
like someone trampling on the arms and legs
of bodies washed up on a beach
with bits of string and grapefruit and dead fish.'
I say all sorts of things.
It makes no difference.
I think of you.
It's you.
It's always you.
That's what they're there for,
it's for, he's for, I'm for, we're for
– always you.

116

Desire's a Desire

It taunts me
like the muzzle of a gun;
it sinks into my soul like chilled honey
packed into the depths of treacherous wounds;
it wraps me up in cold green sheets
like Indian squaws
who wrap their babies in the soft green sheathes of irises
that smell of starch;
it tattooes my shins;
it itches my thighs
like rampant vaginal flora;
it tickles my cheeks
like silkworms munching mulberry leaves
on silk farms;
it nuzzles my plucked armpits like fat dogs;
it plays me
like a piano being played
by regimented fingers
through pressed sheets;
it walks across my back
like geese at dawn,
or the gentle manners
of my only nurse,
who handles me like glass, or Bethlehem.

My skin is white.
I neither eat nor sleep.
My only desire's a desire
to be free from desire.

Do It Again

I like the feeling.
Do it again.
No, don't.
It ripples like the soft fur of the tapir
of rhinoceros-family fame,
that feeds on sprouts;
or the rug I smuggled three live ducks for Mother in
on Eastern Airways;

but all we're allowed's anxiety like fishbones
lodged in our throats
as beauty parlours hum;
all we're allowed is having pretty faces
and cold and glittery hearts like water-ices.
Mine's more like a centrally-heated boiler-room,
evil and warm;
like kidneys on a plate.

But all we're allowed's the dry hum of the driers;
all we're allowed's one word,
like darkness:
No.

Me

If the man mending fences
had seen a big familiar girl with bloodshot eyes
heading across the pasture
towards the woods;
if her skin was yellow and blotched,
and something was wrong with her legs;

and if she was being squawked at
by a flock of turkeys,
a pen of pheasants,
and a pen of quails;
by a retinue of abandoned peacocks
from a cedar tree,

who have travelled in a crate
all the way from a Florida orange grove
to a Georgia cattle farm,
only to be walked out on again;
whose Mother was yelling *Where the hell has she gone?*
it was me.

And where was I going,
and why was I going there,
my heart like a sump,
to the woods of the hawk and the fox,
the opossum and snake,
to sunsets playing like organs,
stubborn
and radiant?
You.

I Want To Be Alone

I want to be alone with my duck,
who won the hearts of the nation's good-natured women
with his little irregular snuffles
like mice in bags
as I wheeled him round the lakes
in his sprung pram;
and with my goose,
out hiking in the rain again
among small cattle;
and you, my swan, with your fine taste in snow-white linens.

I want to be alone with my quails.
I want to be alone with my Startena.
I want to be alone with Calomel.
I want to be alone with the Sword
that cuts, that Christ has said He came to bring.

What Do I Really Want

My one-legged, mown-down peacock,
Limpy's sleepy.

Memories of you
are sleepy too.

What do I really want?
Bejewelled jodhpurs?

Peace of mind
is the correct answer.

Sister

Peace of mind is the correct answer.
National Chicken Week is the correct answer.
Roy Rogers' horse attending a church service
in Pasadena is the correct answer;
Banjo, my cherry-red Santa Gertrudis bull with big white eyes
and chubby lips, is the correct answer;
Barred Rockfryers is the correct answer;
their expression of alert composure
is the correct answer;
Equinox, the jackass, is the correct answer;
Lady Bankshire and Herbert Hoover roses
is the correct answer;
Thomas Merton is the correct answer;
The Body of Christ
is the correct answer;
The Instrument of Crucifixion
is the correct answer;
Mother, like butter, is surely the correct answer;
Sister, the Muscovy duck, is the correct answer,
as she flaps consolingly past our living-room window –
Mother's ex-Trappist-Monastery, tough, Trappist-monk of a duck.

AEROPLANES OF THE WORLD

(1994)

For Christy Moore,
from a humble but devoted fan

Being a Wife

So this is what it's like being a wife.
The body I remember feeling as big as America in,
the thighs so far away
his hand had to ride in an aeroplane to get there;
the giggles I heard adults giggling with
I was puzzled about,
and felt much too solemn to try;
buttons unbuttoned by somebody else, not me;
the record-player
neither of us were able to stop what we were doing
to turn off;
the smell of fish
I dreaded I'd never get used to,
the peculiar, leering, antediluvian taste
I preferred not to taste;
the feeling of being on the edge of something
everyone older than us,
had wasted,
and not understood,
as we were about to do;
his pink hand gripping my breast
as if his life depended on it;
the shame of the thought of the mirror
reflecting all this,
seem long ago,
yet somehow authentic and right.
Being a wife is like acting being a wife,
and the me that was her with him in the past is still me.

The Wasps

Our mother liked to feed me perfect veal;
and two invisible drops of Radiostol
were wobbled on my morning toast by Nurse –
a special little wafer, like a host.
She fed my upstairs sister next to nothing.
At least, that's what my upstairs sister thought.
And when I tried to move her head I couldn't.
And when her kitten started licking her,
bit by bit, as if she were a skyscraper
a tiny Tippex brush was painting white,
I ran into the yard to greet the wasps,
and let the licking carry on all night –
my sister on her bed, and me outside,
my naked body smeared with marmalade.

The Man Man

Who is this man?
And why is time different here?

And what does he say,
with his mouth full of *r*s like blood?

He plunges his arms into rocks
and pulls out lizards.

Skinner of swifts,
sucker of brittle eggs,

easer of scented pianos
down warmed ramps,

who is this man,
and what does he promise me?

My mother stops my mouth. She says I must
never never tell him where I am.

My First Bra

A big brown bear
is knocking at the door:

he wants to borrow a dress
and matching knickers.

The smell of lilac
smothers me like wool;

beyond the lawns,
I hear my naked sister

crying in the nettles
where I threw her:

nobody else is having
my first bra.

The Dog-Man

The dog-man from next door has come to play the piano –
to pour out his syrupy notes
like a deluge of ripe, exhausted plums:
they stick in her hair
and mess up her ironed, imported, daisy-spangled cotton dress
that glares out sententiously
like one of those little flower-gardens
harbour-masters and sandwich-bar-owners
dedicate their lives to
with the kind of murderous possessiveness
small seaside towns
obssessed by being the nicest
go over the top with;
she's pressed against by plums as big as radiators,
emperors,
sweating Clydesdales,
suicide,
over-heated Japanese 'bath-houses for sexual relief'
she's read about, and puzzled over and tried not to see herself in –

plums buzzing with bright wasps
that cross and recross the precinct of her chair
like a switched-on electric fence
she can't move through.
Her eyes are glazed,
and her face could be basked on by lizards it's so still.
She's mistress of the art of frozenness,
hiding at the side of herself
like a pilgrim bathing in the Ganges
being cruised past by loudspeaker-toting boats;
like a diseased tomato;
like a brain-damaged child strapped in a van
who's watching, or anyway parked in front of,
an open-air, wrap-around, drive-in,
completely incomprehensible picture-show,
and the van has a sliding door
that might accidentally slither open any minute
and send a whole avalanche of untouchable things
that have no business to be there,
and should never be seen,
tumbling out into the open
like mutes or brains;
and at night,
when I'm nearly asleep,
I sometimes come across her –
vicious, hunched-up and incapacitated
still hugging her hairless awkward little thighs.

Selima Selima

Where does shame come from?
It comes from my hands.
Where does shame come from?

It comes from my name:
Selima, Selima.
My father gave it me.

Where does shame come from?
It comes from a waterfall
somebody's kept for years in a woollen purse.

My Life With Men

The first man I attracted
was my father,
who people said was young:
how young he is!
But actually he wasn't. He was old.
I told my little friends he was the lodger.
Next, the man who called me
Schlobovitz
and worshipped me unstintingly.
They all did.
And then the man I found upstairs in bed,
who said he was my
Unexpected Brother.
Why do people have to lie like that?

And later on I met his friend The Man.
And then another.
I was off my head.
I never loved them but I wanted to.
I wanted to so much I thought I did.
So much, in fact, I even married one,
and went to live in Manland, among Men;
where other women,
wrapped and stunned
like meat,
introduced me to the long machines
we mustn't leave
on pain of death
all day.

We mustn't walk,
or even go outside.
(If anyone's seen 'loose' –
without a car –
they're rounded up
and given clocks and pills.)
We mustn't talk –
except of course, effusively,
every time the phone rings.
Then we must.
(As long as what we say
is not the truth;
as long as who we're talking to's
a stranger.)

Our flowers
are dead.
Our animals
are headless.
Our children
are for smashing against walls.
And when the day
has done the best it can,
with well-scrubbed hands
we set our plastic clocks
and slip
like liners
into dreamless sleep,
remaining almost motionless till morning.

Crocuses

And is her father with her on the lawn?
Absolutely not.
She needs to be quite alone.
And what is she drinking, on the lawn?
Hot tea.
And what is she writing?
Things that have made her angry.
*And has a certain bunch of flowers
made her angry?*
Yes.

He stepped out
into the sunlight,
still in his nightclothes,
and made his way
down the hill
to the orchard.
Her first gold crocuses
were pushing up like fish
(she wanted *no one* to see them)
between striped wasps on plums.

And what sharp implement
was he carrying down with him?
Scissors.
And if he were to cut himself –
remember he's an old man now –
would she come running down the bank with sheets
to stanch the bleeding?
No, she would not.
And will she forgive him?
Never.

Joseph Beuys, Yul Brynner, Sigmund Freud, Gorbachev, Freya Stark and Me

We never mention it,
this secret scar
I was carried in the arms of the farmer
through the roar of burning wheat-fields to prevent;
that smelt like the piglets
left singeing in the hay-barn, screaming like hares;
that drove my mother to carry
painfully expressed breast-milk and sieved carrots
through the streets of the deserted city
at night in little jars, to soothe me with;
that banished me to a childhood
behind muslin;

papery, polished and thin,
like a dried flower,
or the ghostly imprint
of my mother's love,
or lack of love,
or whatever it was
that caused the accident –
so can you pretend, for all our sakes, if you can,
I've got nothing in common
with people disfigured by scars,
especially scars on the head, especially the face,
OK?

Standing Here Beside You

Standing here beside you makes me sad.
You're like a house I watch the windows of

knowing I can never go inside.
I see a woman passing to and fro

and envy her the freedom I can't have.
I only watch. And you?

You're watching too, frozen
in your prison of white flowers.

Milky

We peeled our sunburnt babies
like garlic cloves,

and the slivers of skin stayed where they fell
in air as stubbornly still as vastness and joy

locked in an oven would be;
where only the drip of the milk from your longed-for breasts,

as they pressed against the glass-stiff stiffening
of your Lycra swimsuit cups

like patiently caught fish contained in jars,
moved,

if you call it moving –
seeping, leaking,

giving the room the faint white smell of a dairy
falling asleep like a pear behind closed doors.

Beethoven's Mother

When the glazier
manoeuvres his rectangle of glass
across the street
like a slice of frozen lake,
I think of you;

when small flocks, roaming open fields
in autumn
like freed cyclamen,
on wings as thin as nasal blood-vessels,
sing as they fly,
I think of you;

and when I read that Beethoven's mother,
cooking pastries
in the back streets of Cologne,
'lulls his overwrought feelings
into tranquillity',
of course I think I'm Beethoven, with you.

The Toe

Not long after our late mother's death,
my sisters and myself, weak as we were,

decided to come down off the mountain
and settle ourselves here in the woods.

And if they come, they come. We have no fear.
Something, we're convinced, is watching over us,

something we're too small to comprehend.
All we see's, at dawn, a giant toe

we offer roses to we drag by night
across the heath among the wounded larks.

The Birds

They've closed it down, but someone is alive.
His eyes are watching for a door to move.
Once he saw, or thought he saw, tall women
running down the mountainside with oranges;
once he saw a soldier on a horse
looking up at him in disbelief;
but all he sees today is the road,
glittering and white, between the trees;
and, moving imperceptibly, like clocks,
the giant eyeless birds, unknown to science,
who come to fish on fine days in the lake.

Brides with Songbirds Tangled in Their Veils

As soon as people realised what was happening,
they opened up the mine in the mountains
and turned it into what they called a nightclub,
complete with 'rest-rooms', known as *Darkest Night*.
Not the most inspiring name, admittedly,
but then these people never claim to be.
In fact they're proud of being uninspiring.
The less I have to do with them the better.

I much prefer to go in search of nets –
creeping down the bank beyond the woods
late at night or early in the morning
and pocketing as many as I can
before the sentries wonder what I'm up to,
or, even worse, before the man appears
whose nets, like brides with songbirds in their veils,
I like so much on starry nights to plunder.

Silence

Her path, if you can call it one, is silence,
obviously quite different from our own,
and one, as I have said, that we will monitor.
It's true she makes my people here uneasy –
she makes it hard to go on acting normally,
and not to call in question one's beliefs.
Another thing – her smell of chickenfeed.
To be precise, of chickenfeed and lemon.
Curled up on my eiderdown this morning,
she looked like something put there to annoy me –
and I must admit I felt a strong temptation
to wring her little neck, and dispose of her,
which would have been quite easy in the circumstances,
there being no bright feathers to betray us.

Carnations

And when he died, the reign of brutality and abuse
that had gone on undetected for nearly twenty years
suddenly came to an end;
and we fell asleep among our fathers' horses,
and that's how it all began –
with the sound of their breathing.
They waited by our sides, like aeroplanes,
or graves, enclosed in silk,
dusty and sweet like sponge cakes
or carnations;
we must have lain exhausted at their feet
for many days and nights;
we saw the moon
unroll ten thousand miles of suffering
along their backs, as if the mane of one alone
were Upper Burma,
as if each fetlock were Mongolia,
where there's only fifty miles of tarmacked road,
the rest's small flowers...

What happened next, my friend,
you already know –
something it's hard for the people here to believe,
after the reign of abuse
we've been subjected to,
timid as we are,
for so long now.

Evelyn

All I do's admire the distant sky-line
and run my fingers through the rustly sand
while Evelyn, ever patient and resourceful,
trundles off in search of tasty ants.
And every night, at peace beneath the stars,
we visualise the zoo-man in his bedroom
battling with his large electric fan.
We visualise him getting out of bed
and switching off, not only his supply,
but everyone's. The whole population's.
And everything goes ominously quiet.
Then gradually, as dawn begins to break,
he sees to his astonishment brown animals
shuffling up his drive with their families;
and as the days go by he gets to like them
– in fact he can't imagine ever not.
They fill his house and gardens with their
normalness. Just the way they seem so down-to-earth.

Marguerite

Because of the execution or suicide
of so many of his intimates,

they are looking with mounting desperation
for someone who really knew him –

someone who knew the place
where he held the meetings,

who had seen his face;
someone who fed him,

mashed the flesh of his apples;
replaced his warm lilies;

who tiptoed across the bright fence
in her checked dress

with a convoy of lorries
rumbling through her heart.

That person is me.
But nothing will induce me to come forward.

I will stay here in the ruins of the hospital
with Marguerite, the one I love,

who has not forgiven me for going away before,
and will not forgive me again. Not a day passes

without my sitting quietly by her cage
as if to apologise.

The people on the island bring her meat
caught in the woods for her.

These are the men with disabilities,
who feel respect for such a proud creature.

And those confined to wheelchairs can sing praises to her
streamlined silhouette.

Voices of Bulgaria

He's found a bear the same size as his mother
and walks about the dayroom holding her.
He calls her Marigold. With velvet ears

he hears the yellow sea below the window
rocking on the sand-bar like a horse
lying on its side, that can't stand up;

or like the parrot that he slept beside:
he wrapped it in a scarf with hearts on it,
to keep it warm, but even then it died...

His heavy hand is resting on her dress,
crushing her dumb sleepy whitened roots
beneath the snow, beside the little villa,

where lost mysterious voices of Bulgaria
are heard among the rabbits, quietly singing...
He grunts and ties his hair into a knot.

The polystyrene granules Marigold
was holding back so long come pouring down
like gold and jewels: *Marigold, my love!*

Marylou

She must have been extremely tired that morning,
and, as far as we can picture her today,
she must have been relieved to see the hut
she came to know so intimately later.

He would have been at work on the verandah,
completely dressed, as usual, in brown fur,
his human face half-hidden by his mask.
She watched him for a while, from a distance,

then something scared her, and she slipped away,
keeping close to where the river ran,
and planning to return with reinforcements,
with – sadly, as it turned out – Marylou.

The days that followed must have been the happiest,
certainly the quietest, of their lives –
the flickering fire, the dice, the racks of mushrooms,
the snow that watched them from the porch like dolls.

My Darling Reindeer

I was still feeling wary of humans, as you know,
and my first reaction was one of profound relief.
The sun came out, and everthing went quiet.
Once a tiny aeroplane flew over,
otherwise the only sound was crickets
clicking in the asters like dry nuts.
And then a man appeared, as if from nowhere,
and sat beside us, like a normal man,
like long ago, when there were people here,
and hungry men, and dogs; and crackly radios
competed with the crickets' castanets.

Hundreds of Letters to Hundreds of Naked Men

When he comes home in the evening
and stands in their bedroom
like a police officer at low tide
beside the clock
the thief threw into the sea
he hasn't noticed yet
because of the crabs and shoes and guillemot corpses
like hundreds of strewn-about letters
to hundreds of naked men,
she can't even look
without wanting to shrivel him up;
without wanting her look,
like the relentless sun
that renders bared farms
salt-encrusted wasteland
good for nothing but racing racing-cars on,
to shrivel him up.

But on the day they called him out three times,
as the only practising apiarist in the area,
she suddenly felt as if they had fallen in love,
she suddenly felt as if they were lovers again
(his lip on her neck,
their love in the air like a lark),
but it was no more alive than the dachshund
she met one night in the cul-de-sac,
lark-coloured,
and soft as a bean-pod lining,
that had died there –
everyone knows that –
that had died there,
swaying its final,
disappointed, spurious,
amber sway,
O, *years* ago.

Sparkle

I'm not as unprepared as you might think.
Take a look outside my window. *Dogs.*
All day they wait like soldiers for my voice,
a voice so beautiful that everyone –
no, not so beautiful, a voice so clear –
that everyone who hears it, dogs included,
will leave the hospital, without a fuss,
some with chocolates, some with fish, or fruit,
and make their way into the distant mountains.
And if they want to dress in dresses, let them.

Let them wear the shiniest materials
the nurses and the clergy can provide,
so when they reach their final destination
the rocks will sparkle with them – for one year.
Then men will come, attracted by the light,
and, armed with flames, expertly incinerate them;
returning with the ash to the valley,
where things have changed, and even dogs are burnt,
and palm trees' desiccated leaves go clacketty,
in at the hospital windows, *clacketty-clack.*

The Voice of Bobo

(i.m. the late Bobo, bull terrier)

Everything inside this room is mine.
And everyone inside it has to stay.

It's where I keep my horses and my men,
cooled on summer days by giant fans

whose steady rhythm
calms the anxious mind.

Nor do I want torpor, or docility.
From the very moment I arrive

I like to have each person's full attention,
until a silence is attained so deep

some of you will hear the Voice of Bobo,
when, after having queues of tiresome people

teasing her by blowing down her ear,
she suddenly can't bear it any longer

and starts to bark, as only Bobo can.
Those who hear that precious Voice go forward

to other, smaller rooms, for the Advanced.
Everybody else must stay on here –

here between the land and the sea
where long ago I built this secret palace

balanced on the cliff among the predators
to take advantage of the sweeping views.

Abstract Expressionism

She had this huge dog –
a mastiff, I think it was,
that her father had bought her
when the doctor suggested having a dog might help –
and she walked very fast on her spindly legs beside him,
trying to keep up; she'd come up alongside him finally,
and he'd stare into her eyes
like Wittgenstein.
It was snowing – the sort of weather,
the harbour-master said,
one minute you were wishing you were dying,
the next minute you were wishing that you weren't;
and the girl with the big dog laughed,
although she didn't understand him,
and she was only wearing a cardigan,
so she must have been terribly cold.
Then the harbour-master
invited her into his little office,
where two German tourists,
looking very much at home, were painting the sea.
Was it you who was saying, the bigger one said,
Ad Reinhardt went all the way round the world
and took 5000 photographs – or was it 50,000? –
and not a single one of a human,
not a single one!
Her partner nodded, and gave the dog a sandwich,
and then looked up at the owner,
who got one too.

Night-Night

I met him on the stairs quite unexpectedly,
and there and then I left the little hospital
and, trusting him as much, or more, than humans,
followed him, without a word – to you.
Some of you, I know, have been expecting us,
have waited years, in fact, for our arrival,
so can I take this opportunity
of thanking you for your encouragement?

Your country, as you know, is not well liked,
and anyone who comes, must come alone.
We have to make our way across the mountains
by intuition, some would say mistake,
not really knowing why we started out,
or who we are, or what we're looking for.
It's like the special side-room at the hospital
that patients other patients were unsettled by,
patients needing quiet, used to sleep in.
And people loathed it. Anything but that!
Why? Because it's up a little stair,
and looking out on nothing but the moors.
But once they did, and this applied to everyone,
a subtle transformation would come over them.

Wolves

Normally a rather timid man,
he knew exactly what he had to do –
find a wolf, and, watching every movement,
kneel down before her in the darkness
where endless little bands of beady nightlife
stream like gold across the forest floor
as if there's been some terrible mistake
that only they are able to correct,
only they and those like them who know.
Most of all, he needed to kneel down –
something not encouraged in an office.
Offices are not the place for tiptoeing,
gazing, kneeling, anything like that.
Offices are not the place for wolves,
or anyone involved with them, or night.
Offices are meant for office-workers.
Anybody else will be removed
and flattened out in basements by machines.
Nothing is the name they'll be remembered by,
lots of it, as ordered, nice and flat.

The Island

Men want to understand, and think they do,
and maybe if they don't it's not their fault,
but basically this place belongs to us.
We like to organise ourselves ourselves.
And anyway, anyone can visit –
brothers, fathers, lovers, anyone.
My son comes often; or I visit him.
You ask us if we miss them. Not at all.
We don't use cars, or electricity,
and men especially seem to find that hard.
Another thing – we feel healthier.
We work the horses; bear much fewer children;
and eat and dress and live very simply.
We shepherd sheep. We scale trees for fruit.
We abseil cliffs for samphire and fresh eggs;
and some of us, as you have pointed out,
migrating to the cities, abseil glass.

Heatwave

Only the movement of the occasional rabbit
or the drifting shadow of a distant crow
disturbed the stillness of the marble quarry;
and it must have been nearly an hour, he told me later,
before he saw her, white against the grass –

white as fish-bones,
white as sun-bleached eyelashes,
white as the elongated mother-of-pearl lozenges
cunningly inlaid in the musical cigarette-box of her second home,
white as the hands of the man who delivers her anthracite beans.

What Happens in the Present

Why do they have to have their fried eggs and black coffee and tame maids
and an urgent phone-call to make,
and not enough time to time time?
And are their holidays really relaxed enough?
And are the shops near enough?
And the car servile enough?
And is the moment following the moment
following the moment fast enough?

so they never get touched by the present's immediate present –
where women walk to beaches with white skin;
where the beach-chalets' very decay
lends them an air of sanctity we feel at home in;
where salt smells of salt;
where silk feels like topspin;
where people we pass belong to the same side as we do,
where everyone does;

where a briefcase sits alone in a locked office
as its owner comes crawling along a narrow ledge five storeys up
to get it back, and carry it home through the streets to his strip-lit bed
where bagfuls of kittens mew from nightbound skips;
where someone like me – for the sake of the way things are,
for the sake of the present,
for the sake of its calm, enigmatic compassion –
will die for someone like you.

How To Be Happy

In the crowded hold of someone's boat,
chocolate sauce is being poured on pears
that shudder as the chocolate coats their shoulders
and spreads its lip across each tilted plate,
across the laps of guests, the rubber floor,
till everything is sunk in utter darkness,
and no one speaks, and no one even moves.
Years go by; then someone's eyes make out
the polished surface of a chocolate sea
where tiny golden boats are busy fishing.

Boating

Few, if any, went to bed that night,
and in the morning rescue teams set out.
Only those too weak to help remained –
the little man, the children, three small hens.
They waited in the house for what seemed days
until a river made of melting snow
carried them away towards the sea –
everyone, that is, except the man,
who had a boat, and rowed upstairs to bed,
but even that, his fifty-year-old bed,
slipped away as he approached, like sand,
and then the house itself was washed away,
and he was left to roam the world alone,
rowing through the tree-tops in his nightshirt,
or sometimes rowing, sometimes simply drifting,
feeling too relaxed to really think;
but once he saw a woman dressed in white
waving from the rail of a liner;
but when he called, she didn't answer him –
as if to stop him calling out like that
and spoiling the whole joy of the occasion.

Eating Lychees in South Kensington

Still blushing at the feet of tall men's houses –
fathers' and uncles' chocolate-brown retreats

whose nephews tap the lighted streets, like roebuck
glittering with gold and tangerines;

blonde heirs made of knives for slicing veal;
or trout, that mirror water; polished beans –

she feels, in her pocket, crenellations
of waterfalls that she begins to eat:

their sweet, shelled, oval-headed babies
crush their juicy mouths against her cheek;

and chandeliers, as fresh as shrimps and oranges,
clatter in her jaw; while on the street,

she hears, like falling snow, pink in the sunlight,
the sound of gathering armies' naked feet.

A Nightdress Sprinkled with Fish Scales

After what the family call 'the accident'
my sister brought me here to this small castle
that rises from the shores of a lake
rumoured to be one of the deepest,
certainly the clearest, in the country.
And when I say I fish 'from my bed'
I mean exactly that. Have a look.
Swimming may no longer be an option
but fishing is. I lay them on my bed,
cold and heavy like abandoned guns,
and tell myself how fortunate I am.
The doctor, quite a fisherman himself,
sometimes finds a scale, like confetti,
sticking to my nightdress or my bandages,
and picks them carefully off, like tiny mirrors,
before he turns away to join the swimmers
fanning out across my bedside lake.

Mirabelle

I sit up here and watch them from my window
setting off, in groups of two or three,

across the miles of undulating concrete
to spend the day in what, for them, 's like prayer –

retiring when night falls to giant pipes
that echo to the crunch of broken lambs

and something else I can't identify,
a distant pumping, like machines, or blood.

I watch, and wait for Mirabelle to come,
to press against the chainlink fence with orchids

and show me, in his way,
how much loves me.

We'll lie together like two hired snakes,
our brains as soft as sugar, or the skater

whose lovely fragile bones were ground to powder
and scattered on the sites of his despair.

Brueghel's Helicopter

The trees are white,
the hunters have gone home,
and even the skaters on the distant ponds
have fallen silent in the swirling snow.
The little pig has trotted back inside
and settled sweetly in my arms again;
and as it sleeps, its chin against my chest,
the bewildering adventures of the morning
come rushing back in all their vividness –
the way the mules flickered in the moonlight;
the glimmer of the cockpit in the rocks;
and finally the shock of seeing the pilot,
his chin against the window like white meat.

As dusk, then darkness, fall, and rumours spread,
people start to gather at the inn.
I hear the muffled crunch of their boots,
and then the stamps, as they approach the porch.
The men look cold,
their skinny dogs fed-up.
The only comfort I can offer's tea,
brewed by burning tables and dried flowers.
The piglet in my arms is fast asleep;
and one by one, as dawn breaks with no news,
each man returns for solace to his dreams:
I watch the snow, and dream of San Diego,
sizzling in the sun, and full of schnapps.

146

The Veil

Otherwise the room was dark and empty,
except for what I took to be the servant,
apparently not bothered by the smell
I noticed straightaway, of blood and bleeding.
Her face was sullen, and she didn't move.
And neither did the rigid man-shaped veil.
After that, I came back every day,
until at last my patience was rewarded.
The veil moved – as if some furtive moths
were arguing among themselves like thieves.
As morning broke, I crept a little closer;
then, just as I was leaning down to speak,
the servant gave me one of those bleak looks
the neighbours have been paralysed by lately.
Not only you, my friends. The whole area.

A Cup of Kindness

Reindeer calve; the dotterel
sings in the sedge like tin;

small Lapps net chard, and white milk
mixed with sorrel sours in kegs;

a baby, sucking bones in a willow-bush
is dreaming in a world of fur and cloud;

while, overhead, two patient botanists
try and remember the words of *Auld Lang Syne*.

Our Lady of Snow

The person in front of her's blood
continues to drip. The last thing she ate,
or anyone else in the party,
were the little roast breasts of a songbird
aeons ago. Her remaining arm
is difficult to move. She wonders
if they're trying hard enough. Or maybe a rescue
is somehow no longer the point,
and even those in pain – it's conceivable –
imagining the faces of their relatives,
the hospitals and diets and machines,
would rather stay on here in the mountains,
drinking snow, and watching for a plane;
and, as the days go by, no longer watching;
or watching without hope, or knowing why.
Perhaps it doesn't matter if she dies.
Perhaps it means the others will survive.
Her headless body will be rationed out,
to certain people, people who are mobile,
who'll move away, and build a new society,
far from where the rooms are buckled metal,
the beds are other people, or their limbs,
and walking has to be conducted slowly,
like walking with no shoes on on wet fish.

The Villa

His famous cock
that he goes on about's
about as much fun
as a frozen lamb,
and I just ran away
across the heath
one night;
I left the moonlit villa
far behind,
the helicopters, chainsaws,
parrots, knives,

and little maids who specialise
(he gives them sweets)
in screaming
at the parrots;
I slipped away,
and came back
here,
to you:
breathing gently
like a giant flower
smelling of custard
being stirred,
and licked –
custard
made of eggs
and warm vanilla pods
where egg-white islands
shunt
their sugar bays.

Orchids

The aeroplane must have been there
for several weeks. A few birds
were absent-mindedly picking through
the mangled remains of small children,
and a gold dog ran in and out
of the empty cabin, cradling
a spotted quince in its mouth.
The man we were looking for
was lying on a day-bed
under a red tree.
He seemed to be having some problem
with his skin, and was wearing
a pair of white silk gloves
and a white blood-stained hat.
He was the only survivor able to speak
and even he was too weak to talk
for more than a few minutes at a time.
He was an ex-oil-pipe-contractor
and a millionaire

who had been looking for a place
to breed orchids ... and as he spoke
he lay back on the bleached canvas
of his ancient bed,
his eyes beginning to run,
his limp white penis
resting in the sunlight
on his glove. While my colleague
went in search of a blanket,
I listened to the gunfire
from the valley,
where my daughter lay awake
behind closed curtains
guarded by sweet machines
like a rare flower.

The Runway

As days, then weeks, went by,
my fears increased.
Once a hare was taken from a trap;
once I heard the crunch of a boot.
Finally, late one afternoon,
walking back along the upper bank,
I saw a swimmer swim across the lake.
I watched him for a little while in silence,
then gathered stones and stoned him steadily
until he disappeared without a trace,
and silence re-established itself –
silence, and the memory of Mother,
zipped up in her nylon sleeping-bag,
dragging herself slowly like a foot
across the tarmac with a scraping sound.

VIOLET

(1997)

MY SISTER'S SISTER

My Sister's Tooth

I watch for her until she's really there,
crossing open fields strewn with limbs
she has to pick her way through very carefully
in order to get safely home to me –
me, a little girl in yellow shorts
waiting for the tooth she promised me,
a human tooth embedded in a bean
and carved into the shape of a poodle.

My Sister's Nose

Everybody marvels at her nose.
It's beautiful and slender, like her mother's.
I, her younger sister, marvel at
the way she talks to men I do not know.

My Sister's Kitten

Our mother likes to feed me perfect veal;
and two invisible drops of Radiostol
are wobbled on my morning toast by Nurse –
a special little wafer, like a host.
She feeds my upstairs sister next to nothing.
At least, that's what my upstairs sister thinks.
And when I try to move her head I can't.
And when her little kitten starts to lick her,
bit by bit, as if she were a skyscraper
a tiny Tippex brush is painting white,
I run into the yard to greet the wasps,
and let the licking carry on all night –
my sister on her bed, and me outside,
my naked body smeared with marmalade.

My Sister and I Visit the Zoo

My sister kindly takes me to the zoo
where very soon I get completely lost
and spend the day waiting in LOST CHILDREN
until my sister comes at closing time,
neither of us having seen the animals
whose smells like buns I carry carefully home.

My Sister and I Go on Holiday

A spotted dog is struggling to give birth
and someone in a lacy shawl is waving
but, hidden in our hats, we hurry on,
not forgetting, in her hand, the knife
our doctor has insisted we take with us.

My Sister's Hats

She stands beside their open cars at night
posing like a llama in a hat –
sometimes white like felted piano keys,
sometimes crinkly green and blue like money.

What Does My Sister Do Behind Her Door?

She catches angry wasps in blue glass jars,
she stows a sum of money in an owl,
she slides a folder underneath her bed,
breeds unwanted kittens, ripens plums;
she thinks about her sister hiding somewhere
scribbling in her notebook like a spy,
she thinks *she thinks she loves me but she doesn't,*
she doesn't understand a word I say;
she waits until the cars have driven off
then quickly gets undressed and goes downstairs.

My Sister Goes to Italy

My sister can't decide which to choose.
First one, and then the other, take her out.
Finally the problem is solved:
she gets engaged to both of them at once.
When little Bee and six-foot Boo find out,
my mother puts a notice in *The Times*,
packs her bags, and takes her off to Italy –
leaving me to feed the seven kittens,
and sex them with my finger in their fur.

My Sister Has Twins

The twins are sleeping soundly
in the nursery
while out beyond the car park
in the sun
their mother
in a nightie and a duffle coat
is catching
the first bus to the sea.

My Sister's Poodle Is Accused
of Eating the Housekeeping Money

Everybody's standing in the kitchen
staring at a normal-looking dog
that actually, according to my sister,
contains the missing twenty five-pound-notes.
We stare at it some more.
It doesn't move,
taking neither one side nor the other.

My Sister Says She Wants to Play the Piano

The trouble is she has to be alone,
so here we are, trooping round the fields,
dressed in aprons, towels, indoor slippers,
pretending we can hear determined practising;
in the dappled drawing-room, meanwhile,
the piano sleeps as soundly as a fish
dreaming of the day it rolls over
and floats away indifferently downstream.

My Sister's Dress

Down she comes,
her hair a strange yellow,
her little dress so tight
she can't sit down.
But where does she go to?
And why does she go for so long?
Nobody knows,
and nobody wants to know.
Perhaps a storm has swept the bridge away,
perhaps she's sick,
perhaps obeying orders –

stealing carp,
mutilating horses,
running baths
for lonely heiresses.
But do we ask her
in the morning?
No. Everyone just stares at her,
like idiots,
as, half asleep, she floats
across the lawn
in clouds of lace
and minuscule high heels.

My Sister on My Wedding Day

She slips into the bathroom during breakfast
and nothing will induce her to come out
till finally I have to dress downstairs.
Actually I like it. We all do.
We like her being locked in a room
softening and warming herself.

My Sister and I Have Breakfast

She spoons the fruit between her teeth like jewels,
cube by peeled cube – trickling juice,
and letting the long sleeves of her nightdress
fill the air with time like a vat
round and round whose brittle rim the ambulance
calls the faithful to their red ice-cream.

My Sister and I Finally Arrive at the Hospital

She sweeps onto the ward like a bride
with armfuls of white nighties and fresh flowers
that beam *Come on.* My sister beams *Get back.*
You mustn't touch. You mustn't speak to her.
Or even look as if you're able to.
You have to stand where I can see you, Darling,
but not too close. And never say a word.
But, very quickly, once, I risk a whisper.
My mother whispers back. We both agree
it won't be long before she dies. However
my sister must be humoured till she does.

My Sister Leans Over the Bed

When I see her take your hand like that
something heavy like an unwashed fish
rises to the surface of my skin
and drags itself about, as if it's lonely.
Mother – I'm not thinking of you.
I'm thinking of the safety of the Ladies.
Of standing by the sinks with nothing on
and refusing to open the door until I'm clean.

My Sister and I in the Lift

Every day I dread stepping out.
I dread the ward. I dread the corridor.
I dread the sight of seeing her in bed.
I dread the rush of sweat inside my clothes.
I dread the hours of having to be brave.
But failing to be brave would be much worse.

Or maybe failing's being braver still.
Can everybody please leave the ward.
I want to be alone with my mother.
They lost her in the bowels of the hospital.
She waited in her wheelchair all day.
My sister must be bodily removed.
Injected with a sedative if necessary.
The two of us are sisters it is true
but have you noticed how we never speak?
We used to have a doll called Violet
that used to smell of violet cachous.
Or did I just imagine it? The kisses?
Did I just imagine those as well?
Give us back the bald velvet face
stuffed with straw that creaked
when we cuddled her, give us back
the cheeks we kissed to shreds,
so we can learn tenderness again.
Please remove all the other patients,
or let them die, if they want to, too.
Bring them wild flowers. Nothing else.
Listen to them. Listen to them. Listen to them.

My Sister's Doll

She dresses her in dresses like a doll,
and tries her out in different positions,
as if she's still alive, which she's not,
or barely is, or won't be by tomorrow:
but still she tries to prop her up and feed her,
to think it won't be long before she's home,
before she's reunited with her horses,
before we hear the thundering of hooves,
the roads crack open, hospitals collapse,
and beds emerge in hundreds from the ruins
to flap and honk their way across the sky.

161

My Sister's Secret Rule

My sister has a secret rule: *pretend*.
Pretend we are two normal human beings.
Pretend we are too well-brought-up to lie.
Pretend our mother's feeling *twice the person*.
Pretend we are not lost. But we are.
The falling snow may smell of violets
but it is falling snow nonetheless.

My Sister's Horse

She drives until she can't drive any more.
And then she drives some more. And then she stops.
She thinks she can't be seen but she can.
I'm watching her reflection in the mirror.
It slips into a shop and buys a paper
and reads it in a corner like a thief.
Then hides it in a box of tennis balls.
But why is she so secretive about it?
And why does she keep asking me for cash?
And why do I keep saying *Yes of course*
and why can't people look her in the eye?
And why can't I? And where are all my friends?
And why can't they be told our mother died?
She died this afternoon like a lamb.
We left her covered up on her bed,
took away her things in a bag,
and tipped the flowers into a litter bin.
My sister's gone all tall like a nail.
The mirror's playing tricks on us, I see.
Now she reappears as my sister,
slides a tub of ice-cream on my lap,
changes back into her driving shoes
and drives away as fast as she can.

My Sister and I Meet on the Stairs

She comes up very close,
then turns away,
and, as she turns, she whispers *You killed her*
before retiring stiffly to her room
as if she never said or thought anything.

My Sister's Sister

Every night before I went to sleep
I wrote about our day at the hospital,
and what I hoped, and what I feared, and why;
I wrote about the flowers by her bed,
her cards, her pills, her weight, her temperature,
everything, in fact, except my sister,
or anything connected with my sister.
I do not want her in my private books
where everything exists because of me.
I do not want her rootling around
as if she has to stay because she's true.

The Night My Mother Died I Dreamt of Sailors

I dreamt of sailors sailing past an island
and being startled by the sound of paws
scraping inconsolably on concrete
as animals that used to live in luxury
in special villas cooled by giant flowers
find themselves abandoned by their keepers
and having to survive on dry roots.

My Sister's Horse

She gazes at her body in the mirror,
then gets undressed, and gazes again;
she feasts her little arms on chilly lotion
that wriggles in her palm like chocolate crème;
she plucks her fuzz, she dusts her crevices,
she sucks her razored shins' vermilion nicks;
she seals letters, doctors photographs,
slithers hairless kittens down her bed,
she sniffs her cache of violet cachous
and scans the sky for signs of airborne men;
she feels envy, like a swimming pool,
its room-sized weight, weighing down her room;
and as she falls asleep she hears a racehorse
breathing in the dark outside her door,
the hole that someone's cut into its neck
expanding and contracting as it breathes.

My Sister and I Go Shopping

I offer, first of all, of course, to pay.
To give my name. My sister's. To explain.
To do whatever I have to to get out,
to soften the heart of the man
who grips her arm,
crêpey now and grey like wrinkled stockings,
that used to peek out
from the puffed sleeves
of her pink angora cardigan
so sweetly
long ago –
before she changed,
before it got so cold,
before we got involved in this stupid funeral.

My Sister and the Vicar

Absolutely not
the vicar says,
drawing on the only cigarette
ever smoked inside our mother's house.
My sister understands.
The vicar smiles,
moving on to chocolate-coated cakes.
But on the very morning of the funeral,
she bicycles alone to the village
and, with the help of two confused fishermen,
moves the altar back to where it was.
Back to where it was, like a ship
on its way to where the world ends.

My Sister's Jeans

My sixty-year-old 'forty-year-old' sister,
whose head I dream of floating muslin over,
acres of it, drenched in chloroform,
comes teetering down from the bathroom
in clouds of talc
where what she has done she has
squeezed herself into some shorts
so shockingly short they extrude her like polystyrene,
gleaming, insistent, discoloured, and up to no good,
and reeking of something,
and stuffed full of something alive,
of eyeballs, ferrets, cheeses, swelling hymns,
that she could no more come and sit down beside me in,
no more sit down anywhere in,
and become my sister again,
than a beautiful woman,
whose naked and suckable nipples probe the air
can shimmy up against a wall of mouths
and not be unstable.

My Sister Wants a Muff

My sister wants a muff,
a Persian cat,
a peach, a pool,
a white jardinière;
she wants a little car
to run around in,
a moor, a gun, a lover, HRT,
but most of all she wants my late father –
the way a chandelier would a cosh:
to smash itself to bits with late at night
when everybody else is making love
at lots of deeply satisfying angles.

My Sister's Shoes

Why are her shoes so tight and uncomfortable-looking?
Why are her eyes so big and her waist so small?
Where are her dogs, and why are they all chained up?
Who was she with, and why was he holding a gun?
Who is her father, and why is he never around?
And what does she want? And why is she dressed like that?
And who does she scream at? And why does she scream at me?
And what do I feel? And what do I think?
Estranged.
My sister and myself are *estranged.*
We sit apart and sulk like skinny vultures
growing old together in one cage.

My Sister Loses Her Temper in a Room Full of Children

The children hold their dolls and watch me cry.
And then I feel my daughter take my hand
and lead me up to bed,
to counting sheep,
to dreaming in the little painted bed
the children are still playing with downstairs.

My Sister Calls Me Darling

It isn't really me
she calls Darling
but another, better, sister
she's invented
who lies and steals
and takes our mother fishing
and shakes her senseless
by the gleaming lake –
vicious daughters
red of lip and hair
who top her up and top her up with morphine.

My Sister's Head

You can't come in, it says.
There's been an accident.
So back I trot,
past the famous roses,
past the gate,
past the sign we painted –
directing neither no one to no accident
nor me to what I've got to learn's not home.

My Sister Has Visitors

When the men from the city,
weighed down by documents and unsuitable clothes,
finally arrive,
my sister hands round various improvised bats
and herds them into the barn to play pingpong
till one by one they sink into the straw
where cows with squints force tongues inside their ears.

The Meeting

When we met that evening on the stairs,
the evening of the day our mother died,
she looked at me as if she didn't know me,
as if she was already out of reach,
someone years of pain had made untouchable,
had dipped in glass for their own good.

My Sister Goes to London for the Day

The only sign of life is one old dog,
black and white, chained to the gate.
Someone he once knew when he was young
unclips the chain and puts him in a van
and takes him to a new, and kinder, home.
Or does he think his owner will come back,
the one he used to have, before the chain,
and, finding him no longer at the gate,
does he think he hears her calling him?
And in the evening, when he doesn't come,
does she leave a door slightly open
before advancing with a shrimping net
alone across the heath to catch him hares?

Giant Cows

It's in a dream but they don't know it yet.
Sunlight bathes the children on the lawn.
Everyone is dressed in white and laughing.
The giant cows are paddling in the stream.
Smell the lilac. Smell the famous roses.
It's in a dream. The dream has got it wrong.
I look at her and realise she's the one.
I have to go immediately. *Forgive me.*
Afraid, polite, my mother will obey.
She does not know that childhood is over.
She does not know my sister is the one
I want to be contained until she's still,
I want to be absolved, like a moth,
I want to be absolved and pacified,
softened, crumbled, charred and turned to powder,
I want to say *it's over* to, and touch;
but in the dream it's only just begun.
It looks as if it's perfect but it's not.
I watch them as they laugh and drink their tea
as if they're Them, like That, and never won't be –
and walk away, unable to explain
the day's a dream but they don't know it yet.

My Sister's Christian Name and the Word Darling

Certain words I know I shouldn't use.
Fucked-up liar. Crêpey. HRT.
I know I shouldn't. But I sometimes do.
Other words I ought to use I can't.
I grab at them and whack them on the head.
Otherwise I know I can't think straight.

I Am Hers and She Is Mine

When I was young I knitted flocks of sheep.
I kept them like an army on the landing,
drilled to watch her door, and storm her room,
reporting back on everything they saw.
And in the winter as the days drew in
I knitted every sheep a little cardigan
to keep them warm at night while they waited.
They waited. But she never came back.
She went away to be a grown woman.
Our partnership however gathered strength.
We spent our lives perfecting being enemies
and now it's automatic: I am hers
and she – whom now I only meet in dreams,
with painted face and dogs on chains – is mine.

MY HUSBAND'S WIFE

Why I Left You

When you had quite finished
dragging me across your bed
like a band of swaggering late-night removal men
dragging a piano
the size and shape of the United States of America
across a tent,
I left the room,
and slipped into the garden,
where I gulped down whole mouthfuls of delicious aeroplanes
that taxied down my throat
still wrapped in sky
with rows of naked women in their bellies
telling me to go,
and I went,
and that's why I did it,
and everything told me so –
tracks that I knew the meaning of
like the tracks of a wolf
wolf-hunters know the exact colour of
by the tracks of the tracks alone.
You get a feeling for it.
You stand in the garden at night
with blood getting crisp on your thighs
and feel the stars spiralling right down
out of the sky into your ears,
burrowing down inside your ears
like drip-fed needles
saying *Get out. Now.*
By 'you' I mean me.
One of us had to:
I did.

Those Little Fish

Those little lop-sided fish
that ply gravely up and down
the tiny oceans of propelling-pencils
dreaming of the day
they're called upon to deliver speeches
to hundreds and thousands of wide-eyed
propelling-pencil manufacturers
clinging to rafts,
speeches that are almost impossible to make out
because the waves are so big,
and their mouths are full of water,
and they're facing the wrong way,
and anyway they only speak in
fish language,
those little fish –
OK they're dumb –
can be encouraged;
but you,
even though I lay awake beside you
on rumpled coats
night after night
willing you to make
some little sign, some little squeak,
to squeak back to,
to be understanding of,
to apply my battery of dictionaries
and manuals and tracking devices
and calibrated sensors to,
don't even dream
that you speak.

Please Can I Have a Man

Please can I have a man who wears corduroy.
Please can I have a man
who knows the names of 100 different roses;
who doesn't mind my absent-minded rabbits
wandering in and out
as if they own the place,
who makes me creamy curries from fresh lemon-grass,
who walks like Belmondo in *A Bout de Souffle*;
who sticks all my carefully-selected postcards –
sent from exotic cities
he doesn't expect to come with me to,
but would if I asked, which I will do –
with nobody else's, up on his bedroom wall,
starting with Ivy, the Famous Diving Pig,
whose picture, in action, I bought ten copies of;
who talks like Belmondo too, with lips as smooth
and tightly-packed as chocolate-coated
(*melting* chocolate) peony buds;
who knows that piling himself stubbornly on top of me
like a duvet stuffed with library books and shopping-bags
is all too easy: please can I have a man
who is not prepared to do that.
Who is not prepared to say I'm 'pretty' either.
Who, when I come trotting in from the bathroom
like a squealing freshly-scrubbed piglet
that likes nothing better than a binge
of being affectionate and undisciplined and uncomplicated,
opens his arms like a trough for me to dive into.

Buckets

I came home from work
to find my kitchen had been completely taken over
by two strangers
who had decided to use it
as a field hospital,
and one was the wound
and one was the wounded patient,
and I was to be the orderly, apparently,
shifty-looking,
wearing enormous shoes,
who used to live with finches
like a finch,
whose kitchen
was a finches' wonderland;
who drags her mop around the coughed-up blood
clattering buckets
like a complete idiot.
And she is the blood
and you are the blood-stained patient
who's coughed her up
in the flightpaths of my joy.

Being Fifty

Being fifty makes me feel large,
large and cold
like someone else's fridge.
I harbour scarlet fish
and fat gold eggs
that men in suits
with hands like vets'
remove.
I never speak.
Sometimes I might hum.
Or very rarely
raise a strangled gurgle
as if I'm trying one last time to lurch forward,
to get my fluff-clogged ankles

free from the lino,
hone myself, develop a fluked tail,
acquire a taste for frogbit,
and push off –
paddle off across the world's wide oceans
like a flat-footed sofa
that's suddenly learnt how to swim,
piled high with jellies, cheeses, cushions,
fishes, poodles, babies, balding men,
swimming-pools, airing-cupboards, hospitals,
and tiny pills, like polystyrene granules,
people advise one, or not,
to start taking.

Your Girlfriend's Thigh

I've got what feels like a cross between
a family saloon car and an eel
the size and texture
of your girlfriend's thigh
lodged inside my stomach day and night
and what I want for my birthday is an avenue
wrapped in gold and silver and so long
the trees, let them be poplars, turn to dots
for me to watch her disappearing down.

How to Kill a Wolf

Being a wife is being good like me.
She doesn't lodge herself
in other people's ears
and grow and grow her dead-straight
headless stalks until your skull's
so full of yellow crops you keel over.
A wolf can get a seed in its ear
and die within a week:
it keels over.
She's like a seed.
Her polished hair's the sort
for slipping into hotel dining-rooms for dinner in
– dead straight.
She's slipped inside.
I am observing her.
She goes about her business like Van Gogh.
If anyone stopped her now
she'd cut their head off.
Do you know that?
It's like he said.
It's like a bad dream.
She's only happy when she's short of time.
If you say a word about the future
she'll gag you with her sulphurated veil.

The Fish Hospital

It's all very well you
shouting at me like that
and trying to get me to answer
your endless questions
but what you don't seem to realise is
that my head –
just as I thought it couldn't be
stretched so tight,
and feel so cold,
and creak like ice,
one minute longer –

178

has turned itself
into a goldfish-bowl
I have to use all my powers of concentration
to keep balanced,
and keep quiet,
for the sake of the fish
that squirm about at the bottom
in not enough water
like lips and tongues
being buried alive under snow,
that are struggling to cry,
but they can't,
they're not formed properly,
while outside in the fields
windswept nurses,
standing in the snow
in their dressing-gowns,
have finally given up waving
they're so cold.

Jesu's Blood

I've sawed it through the throat with a carving-knife –
I'm talking about my platinum ex-wedding ring –
I've made it sharp and jagged like a star
minnows and pixies would use –
you wouldn't get that –
the colour of heart-broken nights
and spinach-leaf veins.
I'm trying not to send it back. I won't.
I won't be angry. Can you understand that?
I see my job as making people happy –
writing little cards and wrapping gifts
in twists of sugared-almond-coloured wrapping-paper.
Wrap it up in Jesu's blood more like.
You can't buy Jesu's blood at Debenhams.
Debenhams is where ex-husbands go
to furnish their ex-wives' exhumed ex-bedrooms.

Red Cows

I remember the day we got married.
Very nice.
Prettiness was all I thought about.
It never entered my head to think about *you*.
Who were you?
Were you there?
I can't think why.
I must have told you *Marry*
and you married.
I must have told you
spend the whole week crying.
I gave you food
you didn't know how to eat.
I gave you tears
you didn't know how to shed.
I gave you the moon
like a cold disc on our bed.
We journeyed on,
two white and lonely ships
shifting our consignments
through dull oceans
only crossed
by those who had lost their minds,
who dreamed they sighted herring-gulls
and coconuts;
who when they woke,
a million miles from anywhere,
saw herds of red cows
running down a mountainside
with their tails stuck up in the air
who they thought were their friends.

Nuage Argente

Nuage Argente –
the name of the house
you betrayed us in,
sucking each other to bits
like two chunks of chopped fish
made fat from feeding on the blood and tears
of other people's partners
and your own.
What a noise
you must be making
behind the curtains
in the little room.
You sometimes soak the sheets.
You sometimes lie.
You 'can't believe you did this'.
Nor can I.
Every day I'll dip you in my syrup.
I'll dip you in and force you to be lovable
and roll you around
in trays of hundreds and thousands.
The lowest of the low my mother called them,
men who messed with other people's wives.
Today's today.
It will not come again.
Somewhere in your heart
there must be tenderness.
If you've got one.
Which they say you have.
You know how farmers
run their hands through grain
to coax large animals to come to them?
I'm running my words
through buckets of prayers like that
to coax something out of the dark
to come and save us.

My Happiest Day

My happiest day was not my wedding day.
My happiest day
was the day we all played baseball
after exams were over
out on the baseball pitch,
I had been lying all night
with encyclopaedias piled on top of me
'to strengthen my limbs'
and I had come out onto the pitch
in the immaculate Jerusalem-white clothes
I had spent all morning
cleaning and pressing and peeling on and off,
and when the ball came sailing out of the clouds
towards my hands
I was the one who caught it –
my hands,
like laps,
or home,
barely touching its belly
as I guided it out of the sky.
Mother Maria yelled *Catch*
and I caught it every time.
So what's so great about catching a baseball ball?
What's the use of being so happy then?
I've got to concentrate on catching everything
you and the world and its wives
and various pungent mistresses
care to throw at me now,
aged fifty-one.
And Mother Maria's got nothing to do with it.
She probably never even touched a man.

Ice

Can't she see she's blocking out my light,
can't she see that everything she does
is blocking out my light
like little kings
I duck and duck and feel exhausted by
that smell of her
and make me so uptight
I'd rather be a wall than a wife
and then I would not have to hear the plop
of ice-cubes in her double gin?
Forget it.
'The little things.'
Her little scarf.
Forget it.
She smiles and says she likes my dog.
Forget it.

My Wedding Ring

I hammered it out like a palette-knife,
flat, for a minnow,
(you wouldn't get that)
or a shrunken platinum plaque
with your love message still engraved on it
in barely-visible loops
as if the dried bodies of sea-horses
had journeyed from a sea
you couldn't even look at without swimming in
it was so blue –
and now you say you don't know what I mean.
I'm not surprised after last night.
I've never been so close to another woman,
a woman brimming over with the details
my 'real' friends were kind enough to spare me,
brimming over like the sandwich box
of maddened wasps
you left on the cooker that night
till the plastic started to melt
and stick to their wings,

and I scraped the whole singed tangle into the sink,
and some of them were trying to clamber out –
and I'm trying not to post you back your ring,
make a little parcel of it for you,
tissue-paper, bows, a little note.
But what's the use? You wouldn't understand.
I might just as well post you
this sudden undignified craving
for tinned milk
I keep giving in to, and sucking,
like *Who shall I cling to,
who shall I cling to now?*

Her Little Turquoise Scarf

When I found her little turquoise scarf
I got a pair of scissors from the drawer,
split her little turquoise jungles open
and sent her parrots screeching to the door.

Green Glass Arms

I wanted them to lock you in a palace;
I wanted dogs to find you there years later
with eggs she has thrown at you
caked all over your face
and doors smashed open
and lights ripped out of their sockets
and all that billing and cooing
that made you sound like unrepentant turtle-doves
with fire-engines embedded in your throats
you couldn't stop
now stopped for good;

I wanted you to get
so sick of one another
she'd tear you to bits in a rage
and leave the country –
but what I've done's invent myself a parrot,
a very persistent parrot
that has got it into his head
that I have to be taught parrot language,
and all the time that he's trotting along beside me
looking exotic,
or hanging upside-down like someone practising
how not to handle an egg,
he's telling me in no uncertain terms
his mother was a lettuce-coloured ostrich
as round and satisfactory as the moon,
and *yes*, he squawks, he wants to live with me,
and tell me lies, and eat my nuts and oranges;
and in the evenings,
when the sun has set,
engulf me in his wicked green glass arms.

The Man I Never Married

I wrote and told his mother we were married.
What a lie. He never even touched me.
I told her out of kindness, I suppose.
And out of kindness sent a photograph
not of him but of a tennis star
to prop beside her bed above the optician's
she lay and waited for his letters in,
dressed in a fox-fur coat and a pair of spectacles
that scraped against her pillow like a crab.
And when she heard the news,
and saw the photograph,
she dragged her leaking body from the bed –
or would have done if Nurse hadn't held her down.
And very soon, attended by the tennis star,
and wrapped in baby foxes,
she was dead.

A Day in the Life of Your Suitcase

The sun is shining brightly when your suitcase
steps, a little stiffly, from its bed
and hurries down the road to the beach
where suitcases of every description
are leaping up and down in the air
looking like a flock of battered monuments
or bits of bedroom learning how to fly.
And look at yours. It used to be your wife.
Now it's half a suitcase, half a bird,
trying to get its lid to be its wing.
And as it lunges off towards the sunset
it's hawking up a load of old dresses
and sausages and clocks and double-beds
that fan across the heavens like a jumble-sale,
plunging the whole country into darkness.

Being Single

Being single's never being nude.
Being single's wearing hats in bed.
Being single's trying to get to sleep
and constantly being interrupted
by important-looking spiders
marching off
to the best poison shops;
by moths like bats
banging their fat heads
against my pillow;
by bats whose plan
is to station themselves in my hair,
by mean-looking flies
doing their lengths on my window,
and indomitable old cockchafers
rehearsing their clicketty-clacks
at such a pitch
all I want to do is go to sleep
and dream about a woman – is it me? –
running towards you with her arms outstretched
in a little knee-length dress that suits her perfectly.

But no. I can't.
I've got to stay awake.
Every ant in England's on its way.
They're coming in red columns from all sides
driving flocks of ferocious-looking sheep.

The Man Who Said He Had Danced with Twyla Tharp

I'd like to own a shop selling shoes.
Only men's, only certain men's, and only shoes.
I won't be needing men –
the fish on legs
that other people sleep with,
slipping in and out of rippling sheets
accompanied by blunt and jellied bodies
forever searching for an inland sea
they've never been to
yet are homesick for
somewhere in the West beyond wild plateaux
white with driven lilies and warm snow.
I don't know what they do there
when they get there.
Maybe there's a boat,
a small hotel.
Maybe there's a rippling double-bed
on which to start
all over again.
Anyway I've never been that far.
Maybe close. In 1968.
With a man who said he had danced with Twyla Tharp.
OK he was small.
It doesn't matter.
Everyone is on the same side.
What side is that?
Of wanting to be good.
Every day I tell myself *Remember:*
somewhere in your heart
there must be tenderness.
What we've got to do is try and find it.
What we've got to do is find it soon.

Being Angry

How can I reach the small clean rooms
of the former hospital where bees fly in and out
of flowers as big as drawing-rooms
and the lake's so close
you can fish in its lap from your bed
and the residents ask you for nothing,
if asking for love is for nothing,
and even the sand on the shore
is seamlessly gold,
if I won't stand up?
Nothing works.
Nothing makes me move.
I lie here with my eyes all clouded over
and insects sucking
where my legs should be –
and as I speak they're pouring up my arms
and crawling down my throat
as if they own me.

Chocolate Sardines

They tell me to be tough: *be tough*, they say.
Be tough yourself.
I refuse to be.
His favourite food awaits him in the fridge –
his favourite fish,
like his mother bought him –
their silver eyes and eyeball-coloured scales
keeping cool inside its frosty door
like slivers of bright nights
when we were lovers.
Take that back.
Lovers sounds ridiculous.
Nights when everyone else
but us
were lovers.

The World's Entire Wasp Population

This feeling I can't get rid of,
this feeling that someone's been reading
my secret diary
that I kept in our bedroom
because I thought nobody else but us
would want to go in there,
except it's not my diary,
it's my husband,
I'd like you to smear this feeling
all over and into her naked body like jam
and invite the world's entire wasp population,
the sick, the halt, the fuzzy,
to enjoy her.

The Smell of the Women

The smell of the women
you drove all over the country
like pet princesses,
the smell of their bags,
the smell of their leopard-skin-gift-wrapped
powders and creams
from pink boutiques in caffeinated cities
drove me away;
and now I'm here, with me,
where sheets can be as spotless as they please,
and roads are white, unhurried, leading nowhere,
and men are turned to chickens at the border,
except for those like you I turn to marble
to think things over for a million years.

Your Thumbs

Your thumbs, your back, your car,
your girlfriend's car,
like the gristly rocks
banging and rumbling in boiling water
beneath the buried sand-dunes of Siberia,
are what I think of
when I think of you;
but what I want to think of is the man
I want to still be fond of when it's over.

Your Face

I haven't seen your face for so long now
I feel like a small exhausted traveller
who, coming home one evening in late summer
across familiar fields in fine rain,
finds a ruin where her house should be
and no one there to greet her at the gate.

Her Little Turquoise Dress

When I saw her,
when I actually saw her
standing in her little turquoise dress
so close to me
I could have almost licked her,
far from seeing lips
encased in hailstones
containing the splintery bones
of deep-frozen kingfishers,
what I saw was a tiny blue woman
swimming around inside a drop of gin.
And at that moment, by her side, I loved her.
At precisely six o'clock
I *definitely loved her.*
I felt it as an unfamiliar arching,
or stretching, of the roof of my mouth.

Her Little Turquoise Breasts

It's time to say goodbye to your wife.
It's time to chuck me out and say goodbye
and let your mind contain only water
for someone I'm the predecessor of
to float around in in her turquoise bra,
its turquoise cups uplifting turquoise breasts
you obviously can't wait
to make the most of.

The Little Dog

If all the glassy skyscrapers of Chicago
were crushed together in a solid lump
and chilled for a million years
and given legs
and set to walk alone
along our streets,
it would not be as icy cold as you
whose heart is frozen like a little dog
that's lost its way far out on the snow,
and people searched –
it was a much-loved dog –
but long ago gave up
and turned for home.

I Want a Lover

I said *I want a lover*. It's not true.
I'm happy as I am being happy
pretending I'm a large kangaroo.
The males are red – not my favourite colour –
and spend their time boxing one another.
The females are lazier, and lovelier –
our bodies are a misty violet-blue,
and filled with sand, and given useful elbows,
and told to spend the day doing nothing
but munching grass and watching parakeets;
and if we meet a wife, to be encouraging,
and tell her what she hopes is out here is.

Your Blue Shirt

I wonder if you ever still wear it,
and if you think of me when you do,
or are your clothes completely different now,
and does she choose them for you, does she take you
and dress you in fine suits of spun camellias
and ties of intricately-woven ostrich feathers,
do you sleep in sheets of sliced champagne
on beds of solid diamond sprayed with stars?
And why get so upset about a shirt?
Because it made your body feel warm.
It made your body feel like a stone
I like to think I warmed my cheek against.

Following Stars

Following stars and maps
that make perfect sense
or if they don't
it doesn't seem to matter,
roaming the world
with my cargo of notebooks and tea,
with my good-looking parrots and babies,
my good-looking shoes,
I am myself again;
and as for you,
you're better off without me definitely.

Being a Grandmother

First, there is a smell of custard-cremes
baking in a custard-creme factory.
And mixed with that you smell a hint of gorse,
of roasted pods cracking on hot cliffs.
Inhale again, and what you smell is stars.
It smells so sweet you smell a little more.
Be careful though. The scent has strange effects:
everything goes quiet. You stay indoors.
You wash your hands. You smile. You lose your way.
At night you meet small animals in bonnets.
You turn a sort of misty violet grey,
and start to sing. And never stop singing.
Men walk past with buckets on their heads.
Some of them, alas, no longer know you.

Your New Shoes

To her, this must be you being you.
To me, you're like a man who's been undressed
and wheeled away to some remote annexe
where women in white skirts and rubber gloves
plump you up and rouge you like a corpse
then wheel you back into the world again,
complete with hair and teeth and new shoes.

No one Else

When I think of you I think of you
and no one else,
and nothing else matters,
it's warm outside,
I'm giving birth to ducks,
they waddle off,
adorable, ridiculous,
to eat their meals standing on their heads,
then waddle back,
my homing eiderdowns,
to use my new-found mercy for their bed.

House of Cows

Yes, you are invited to a ball
to which not only you
but our solicitors,
our counsellors, plumbers, gynaecologists,
station-masters, fishmongers and bank-managers
are warmly, are lovingly, invited;
and it won't matter in the least to anyone
that all the coloured sandwiches
are falling to bits
and a woman in an Alsatian-coloured dress
is handing round a tray of rotten tomatoes
and guests just stand and stare like blocks of fish,
because we are about to spend the night
dancing like we've never danced before,
dancing till the sun lights up the sky
and anger is no more than some old clock
ringing to itself in ancient ruins
only the occasional large cow
wanders in and out of
munching flowers.

The Man Who Looks for Waterfalls

The little man who looks for waterfalls,
whose ears are long,
whose hands are small and icy,
who's here one minute gone the next like light;
who hides himself in passage-ways
in hillsides
to offer up his face
to wandering snails,
wants to be alone with me. I know that.
To lie beside me in the dead of night
like ash out late shifting its pink fur
on beds of rock we'll watch the moon rise from –
deafened
by the elongated lake
that doesn't know what else to do
but fall.

When He Follows Me into the Café Looking Nervous

When he follows me like this, I want to say –
when he follows me into the café
looking as nervous and excited
as somebody following a river
in search of waterfalls
to slip inside his coat
before they fly out
into the ballrooms of the night
like wild horses
galloping across the sky
with chariots full of fishes
at their heels
dressed in skin-tight
crunchy sequined dresses
that can't stop dancing
faster and faster like Catherine Wheels
for fear of collapsing
down on their knees till they crack
and whisper *do it do it* –
don't be shy.

The Slinky Dress

I would never have written the letter
without the dress
that seems to release me into a kind of heaven
by far the most radiant angel in is me,
darkened only by the large shadows

his hands that track my dress like hunters cast
till I no longer know if it is him,
the slinky dress,
or love itself I love.
Love itself, surprisingly, feels cold.

So if he wants to sleep with me tonight
let him be a tiny naked fish –
or a tiny fish in a T-shirt if he must –
and swim inside my lake of liquid ice
shop assistants kindly sell in TOPSHOP.

The Waterfall Man

I keep them in white lofts like tall pigeons
and train their long brown arms to carry messages
to somebody I know who will have walked
beside the river like the river's groom
for so long now his body will be brown,
boneless, supple, tipped with eyes like sprays
and muscular as otters dipped in glass.
His famous leather boots will creak like ice.
His tongue will have the grace and strength of syrup.

Because of him, because of his bright eyes,
his crunchy fish-and-gravel-coloured boots;
because of water pouring through my nights
with a sound like an endless supply
of crystal-glass sewing-machines
cascading through the sky
still systematically machining the seams
of a thousand taffeta dresses
encrusted with jewels and zips and tight bodices;

197

because he's half a man and half a waterfall
there's no such thing as sleeping any more.
To other people,
he's the Head Librarian.
He stands behind his desk and looks severe.
To me,
he'll always be the small man
who roams the world in search of waterfalls,
a woman's eye-lids tucked behind his ear.

I Will Be Arriving Next Thursday in My Wedding-Dress

I will be arriving next Thursday in my wedding-dress.
I will be arriving next Thursday morning
at seven o'clock
in a white satin wedding-dress
the colour and texture
of one-hundred-per-cent-fit Bull Terriers
that feel like eels;
he will hear me
calling his name across the waterfalls,
and, craning his neck
(he's as small as a small jockey),
he will suddenly see me
staring at him through his kitchen window –
my ankle-length satin wedding-dress
dragged over to one side by a large rucksack
containing nougat, maps
and a rocky island
crossed by the tracks of relays of stocky horses
carrying the world's fiercest
and most nimble seamstresses
towards a bed piled high for him and me
with eiderdowns that hold a million lips
peeled from the heads of skilfully-dried
small lovers.

BUNNY

(2001)

Little Dogs

She feels so proud to be so under-nourished
and not to have her aunts all turning up

with little dogs on leads, and tartan rugs;
she feels so proud to be alone at home

like someone in a hangar after midnight
entrusted with the mothering of jets.

Fun

She wanted fun.
What she gets is tartan,

the classics, and a little wholesome food;
what she gets is toothpaste,

and the lodger,
who thanks You for inventing thighs, O Lord.

Shoes

A row of shoes,
a man in silk pyjamas,

unsettle,
like a necklace dipped in dust,

an absent father,
and the father's house.

Hens

The fridge is full of hens.
It's Friday night.

Her only comfort is the word *vanilla*.
She says it again and again till she falls asleep

She's the only child on earth
who's not allowed ice-cream.

Tulips

What the smell of the smell of her girlfriend's boyfriend's jumper
does to her dreams

is nobody's business but hers,
nor the smell of the lodger

going upstairs with his tulips
and passing her by on her bed like a still-born lamb.

Pyjama-case

A small pyjama-case was all she wanted
but what she gets is this enormous house

where nobody touches
and even the beds are cold

and a silver spoon is the size of a cold lily
and the lodger is wearing a floor-length satin dressing-gown

and the bathroom is panelled with mirrors like flattened eyes
in one of which he watches as she pouts

while posing on the rim of the bath
in a bra with cups the size of elastic pudding-basins.

Angel-Top

She feels lovely
in her Angel-Top

and Slipper-Sox
with pimples like rare fruit

that sparkle in the sky
where Cassiopeia

leaning from her sapphire roost
is calling.

Ponyskin

Sedated and grubby like snow
that's falling apart,

she shouldn't be doing this here
when the lights are out

and the blue of the hall
is the black of a swollen river

and there's somebody padding around in his ponyskin slippers
wondering what on earth is going on.

Passion-Fruit

The passion-fruit resembles
coloured bruises

rolled
into a ball you can suck.

Pool

Athletic and chaste,
she plunges into the pool,

leaving the lodger
alone in the house with the dust

and nothing to shine on or do,
like a chandelier.

House

She sleeps in late
as if the house were hers

but it is his.
She should have been more careful.

She should have been attentive
to his timing.

The fact that she was wrong
and he was right.

PRAWNS DE JO

Because she was wrong,
because it was all her fault right from the beginning,
because she was ashamed of even thinking about it,
and should never have been his daughter in the first place;
because she was ugly
and he was magnificent
and she was the scum of the earth,
it must never be mentioned:
the unforgettable smell of the singeing baby,
the unforgettable sight of billowing curtains like brides,
the cot,
the charred muslin,
the endless procession of leggy inquisitive flies,
the orange buzz of the electric fire,
and how she'd sit for hours squeezing oranges,
and how she'd sit and fan the flies away,
and hurry down the streets with aching breasts
to part the veil of flies to please the doctors,
the orange ash, the orange carrot-juice,
are never to be mentioned. In that case
what is she to do with the head
that has to be oiled and covered and never mentioned,
as crisp as the colour of violets sprinkled with salt
that grow in the dark
to within half an inch of her brain,
as the colour of prawns sprinkled with salt and pepper
and served to the rats at a diner named PRAWNS DE JO;
that somebody feels beside herself with guilt about
and wheels her off to the sun-tanned arms of a specialist
and all she wants is for him to unpeel it off
and patch it up with a patch from the lawn of her leg,
but he's kitting her out with a rat-sized wig instead
that she keeps in a box
like pet pubic hair
she's secretly proud of because she is horrified by
but never wears because what's the use of a head
with a tuft of hair like a hat from a cracker on top
that's always about to come skew and slither off;
and what's the use of a scar if it's not to be mentioned,
and the milling of flies
and the sight of the flame-proof fireman
with a baby slung over his shoulder as if she's a pig?
And what's the use of the hand-knitted matinee jacket
the surgeon had to pick out with a pair of tweezers?

Mussels

What look like mussels
soaking in the sink

is a pair of soiled
electric-blue pyjamas.

Cashmere

Staring ahead like something biding its time
in a cashmere suit still smelling of marzipan

and the smell of the mushrooms her mother said smell of vanilla,
and tiny polished boots like hand-made beech-nuts,

he's waiting in the hall for her return –
if waiting is the word for not waiting,

for wanting her, and more than her, and breathing
very slowly, like an ear-drop.

Lips

She carries them discreetly
past the lodger

who crams them down her throat
like broken glass.

Egg

And when the lodger, on the second day,
asks her if she knows the word *cock*

she looks ahead and simply starts walking,
steadying the word like an egg.

Plums

Like drifts
of soft angora boleros

on little girls
who won't be girls for long,

the heavy plums'
faint dusting of white bloom

intensifies the blue
of their purple.

Vaseline

He climbs the stairs
towards the frosty thighs

thumbs and fingers itch
to prime with Vaseline.

Sheets

The sheets and towels of rented rooms
repeat

a million ways
of failing to say *home*.

Chicken

He's roasted her
a little gold chicken

whose crunchy breasts
he's skilfully removing

and laying on her plate
like roasted crocuses.

Jacket

Slide in the moonlight, arms, into his jacket.
Slide in the dark to the dark mahogany dawn.

Everything is possible. Just do it.
Imagine you're a tidal wave's first lawn.

Bedding

Their bodies hold
the darkness of his room

like bedding
in an empty caravan

where light comes in,
if light comes in at all,

as something matt
that's failed to be blue.

Bolero

Her doting aunt
knitted her a bolero –

a puff of powder-blue,
like thistle-down –

but what she really wanted was a wet suit
made of skintight lapis lazuli.

Everything

She's sitting on the steps in her nightdress
examining an ATLAS OF THE HEAVENS

in whose blue circles everything is possible
by virtue of the beauty of their names.

Roses

The circular blue
of the lodger's

inherited saucers
still burst

with their roses
as if there's no word for *dismay*.

Ultramarine

The china blue
of early afternoon,

being all there is to light,
accedes

to bands of dark
ferocious ultramarine

which nothing
can make waver from their task.

Larches

The garden is no place
for little girls.

Followed to the larches
by his shadow,

she's trying not to have to
hold his hand.

Baby

She wants him to never come down from staying up there
and she wants him to die
and she wants him to not be a man

and she wants him to look like and smell like
someone who loves her –
not someone

who's half not a man
but a baby
too sweet and too sickly to last.

Moon

You wouldn't believe
how still she can lie, like a moon

intent on the study of various kinds of smiling
and how effective they are as ways of suffering.

Stars

The night sky
carries stars between its teeth

like pins in the teeth of a woman
designing a habit.

Balaclava

Because she knows he likes her curly hair
she goes to bed

in a dampened balaclava
like some old ship

that's never going to make it
rocking itself to sleep inside a shed.

Snakes

The elastic jaws
of large disgruntled snakes

that lie in heaps
like soft exhausted mattresses

for whom she designs neat hats
and ingenious leashes

close over polished eggs
the size of sheep.

Sheep

In her dream she's in a greasy flood
and sees a sheep half-way up a tree

and when she waves
the lovely sheep shouts down

Get me a boat and a suitcase
and so she does.

Suitcase

Curls, to him, like weight, are irresistible.
She herself wants nothing more to do with them.

Better far to put them in a suitcase
and get a sheep to row them out to sea.

Cows

They teach her aunt, whose house it is, to moo.
They press against the window and the doors

and trample on the flowers and eat the lawn
and when she lies in bed on summer nights

they wander up the stairs and eat her hair,
and when the lodger comes, they eat marshmallows.

Bulls

Up in the room she watches the headless chickens from
and farmers like bulls shunting bulls into bays
and stuffing the heads of calves into clattering buckets,
by the single bed and the single peeling mirror,

up in the room big butterflies fall apart in
and windows stun the heads of tiny birds,
up in the room you can't hear the aunts and uncles from
calling you down for dinner it is so high –

having first removed her flame-retardant pyjamas
and said a last goodnight to the sky –
she dips her hair into the orange fire
she is old enough now to be trusted *never to light*.

Scarf

A small pyjama-case was all she wanted
but what she got was this enormous house

in which she's hunting for a scarf to wear
out of respect for the death of her late hair.

Home

When she thinks of home, the word *home*
echoes in her mouth

like *the dead*
echoes in the mouths of the living.

Doorway

The doorway where the night comes in in torrents
and keeps the yellow break of day at bay,

the doorway where she doesn't want to hear him from
calling her name as soon as she slips through the door,

doesn't want to feed the tiny face
entangled in her hair like a bat,

the doorway where she tiptoes in in stockings,
her six-inch kitten-heels in her hand,

she darkened once. It was her father's doorway.
He told her she must *never do it again.*

Terrace Gardens

The terrace gardens
where she used to play

have slipped into the sea,
leaving rock

up which a girl in ballet shoes
is climbing,

and slipping back,
and climbing forward again.

Boiled Sweets

He's on the landing sucking boiled sweets
that bleed their coloured syrups

into language
he doesn't know he doesn't understand.

Shimmering Lakes

Her every breath
is a silver hundreds-and-thousand

he crunches and rolls
till their tongues become shimmering lakes.

Sapphire

Sapphire light
is gathering in lozenges

and bouncing through the building
with the speed

of beads of glass
bouncing from an amulet

or rumours
of bright mountains coming loose.

Taffeta

It hasn't stopped raining for days and she's stiff with cold
and the prickly taffeta dress he is pinning her into
and walking her up and down and twirling her round in
sticks like ice against the skinny body
the lodger has himself designed the dress for –

as skinny as a deep-frozen rabbit
that didn't want a dress and wanted fur
and let itself be stripped and given sweets
and didn't want to thaw
and couldn't speak.

Milk

The neighbours and their elderly Retrievers
get used to seeing someone sitting there,

sometimes dressed in nothing but a nightie,
fiercely spooning milk from a tin.

Songbirds

Everything is much too big and fat.
His thumbs are buttocks

and his lips' fat red
is kissing her nipples

as if they were poor little songbirds
being kissed by a man with a plucking-machine for a head.

Shame

Shame,
like a white balloon,

still rolls its cry
from room to dusty room in search of flight.

Dawn

All she can do is be dumb like a baby night
that has no mouth and does not know what language is

and only knows one thing – it is essential
to get to be lighter than night and become dawn.

Wristwatch

She hears the little nights inside it tick
like starless nights in secret ammunition depots

where women in tight curlers on all fours
are falling over themselves to be forgiven.

Aunt Lou's Last Summer

Every afternoon they make her
fairy cakes

as warm and light
as little warm breasts

whose cherries
she can lie in bed and suck,

surrounded by a ring of old ladies
with sifted flour and sugar in their hair.

Help

She knew they'd never help her
if he hurt her

but when he does
she weakens and forgets.

Rain

With a head like a fish with something wrong with its head
and a face made of fins for raindrops the size of eyeballs
and frizzy hair beatified as waterfalls
streaming down her back like liquid fingers

she runs across the lawn and round the house
where aunts like boulders sink in plains of down
and thunder is a mother made of waterfalls
with water arms and water laps and kisses

drowning what he told her to, and forced her to, do, for him, with pain,
in driving rain:
rain is all she wants to feel touched by;
her only rule to spend the whole night running.

Running

The giant rabbit running through the woods
is running through the woods because of her –

because he knows the girl who can't stop running
is nicer than the one the aunts prefer.

River

Having left him alone in the house with that look in his eye
as if he were yearning again for a mother's arms
to come down and save him from what's going to happen next
that nobody else but him must even think about,

she runs like the wind to the rim of the swollen river
that's filling the fields and woods with luscious blue
and doesn't know how not to keep on telling her
nothing else remains now but to swim.

Blancmange

First of all everything goes thick.
Her hands and face are coated in thick glue.

And then she sinks; and then the word *blancmange*
fills the flooded woods with wobbly blue.

Angora

The soothing blob of wobbly blue
turns indigo

and calmly explodes
in tiny angora stars

where coloured pets
collapsing with a puff

are congratulating themselves
on dying happy.

Budgie

They offer her a bowl of warm Bemax
and wrap her in a blanket like a clock

and put her in a room with a budgie
and let her cry until the doctor comes.

Doctor

The doctor says
the lodger says I'm sorry.

But it isn't enough.
It isn't enough, I'm sorry.

How

How –
when she spent the entire summer playing leapfrog there
in her yellow shorts in the blazing sun
because she could get a good run-up
by starting at the apple tree
and flying past the famous Zephrin Druin until,
by mobilising all the precision and nobility
of the experiences of the great and wordless mystics
as she planted her palms on the plateaux of little friends' backs,
she finally landed practically waist-deep in water
because of the river that flowed along by the lawn
called to the presence of something that flew like joy,

of a flyer,
who, twenty years later and diagnosed sick,
by blistering the fingers of the blind
with cigarette-butts as they planned
their perfect suicide and suicides
and prising open the side-rooms' unopenable doors,
soon made new friends –
how could he insist on planting a cherry tree,
or getting her uncle's gardener to plant it for him,
the best and sweetest friend she ever had,
or had till then,
right there?

jamming her brain with cherries like boiled sweets,
her eyes with boiled sweets that couldn't cry
but blazed like stained-glass churches in the wilderness
till somebody's put her away
with the dead-end blind:
She shares a room with a milliner from the Valleys
whose twin has sprinkled quicklime in her eyes.
She doesn't even know what quicklime is.
You can hear her coming from all the way down from the side-rooms
because it is London,
the Sixties,
and she wears bells.

Mercy

The man she shows no mercy to is dumb.
At first he spoke odd words,
like angels coughing –
as if to speak would only hold him back –
and now, when it is obvious she is sick,
he doesn't even bother to do that.

Hairbrush

Anyone who touched her would be sorry
and that's why they've put her away, because they were sorry,
and they've put her away
where no one will see her but nurses
who, seeing her sit here alone with nothing to do,
are standing behind her
ceaselessly brushing her hair –
the most beautiful hair the lodger had ever seen,
the hair of angels,
lovers –

till she panics.
She cannot bear their need to understand her,
she cannot bear their need to get so close,
to fondle her scar
and take off their gloves and explore it
and climb up her hair
and drill through her brain to the sorrow
that never stops trying to snatch at the hands on the brush
as they ceaselessly, ceaselessly brush
her desirable hair.

Arm

Every week a different bored doctor
asks her how she is and gets no answer

and then an arm leads her back to bed
to sleep it off for a million years or more

and nobody comes and nobody mentions the lodger
until it is time for her little injection again.

Lobster

The Common Lobster
is morosely blue,

turning red when boiled –
in disgust

at being lifted
from her massive bed

where being blue
is how to reign supreme.

A Thousand Swifts

Perfect blue
seems to ask a question

but what the answer is
she doesn't know,

or how to ask,
or even if there is one;

and, if there isn't,
can there be an answer,

and can the answer be
a thousand swifts.

Galloping Alopecia

The lodger blamed the Galloping Alopecia
her aunt still nursed behind closed doors
on her;
and he didn't like the way she dropped her Ts
and he didn't like the skin on her heels
and the way she straightened her beautiful curly hair
and jumped on thistles
and didn't come home till bed-time
and came home covered in straw
and befriended dogs
with mud on her skirt and hands like gardening gloves
and the tone of her voice
and the way she said Can I get down
and the way she refused to sit down in his first-class carriage
and refused his sweets
and refused to look up from her beetles
and refused to decide to worship the ground he trod on;
he didn't like her knees like cardboard boxes,
he didn't like the way she'd disappear
as if she was right
and had a surprise for him
and she was the one who was never going to forget,

who witnessed his sorrow,
who witnessed his altered blood,
who came across him stooping in the bathroom
making up secret parcels of wild violets
for who or why nobody dares to wonder.
He chopped their little legs off at the ankles
and bandaged them up in damp cotton-wool.
He laid them out in rows like baby quails
with the backs of their poor little heads out cold on the slate.

Nothing

Because she is exhausted
and confused,

and doesn't want to argue,
and can't speak,

she dreams of nothing
for a thousand years,

or what the nurses cheerfully call
a week.

An Angel with Large Hands

She's looking for an angel with large hands
to take him in her arms
like perished silk

that isn't there,
like air is,
when you touch it;

to take him in her arms
like the evening
the moon discreetly takes from the sun.

Colonnades

Because the sun is much too hot for him
and she is strong and he is skin and bone,

she picks him up without a word and carries him
to somewhere cool the sick like him call home

where old men float down pearly colonnades
or spend whole days like fruit in tiled alcoves

doing without moving and in silence
what can't be done by floating with the living.

Motes

He died because of her.
She was too young.

She should have been attentive to the motes
that crossed his darkened rooms

as if in light;
she should have been attentive to his silence –

the fact that he was wrong
and she was right.

The Room

The room it was her privilege to come down alive from,
the rooms she ran upstairs to in the thunderstorm
to where it was impossible to come back down from
without a choir to guide her;
the room where she thought that what she'd found out was
that all she had to do was shut the door,
the room where the bed and the sweets and the door were all wrong;
the room in the house like a black plastic sack full of starlings
that smelled of sugared almonds and mahogany,
the room where somebody whispers to somebody else
something they don't understand
that doesn't bear thinking about;
the room where you follow the river
and seal the lips he climbs;
the room she wants to make absolutely sure of one thing about,
the room where it was like if you go for the door
he'll get you and chop your head off;
where this one thing is the only thing worth living for,
where this one thing's not even worth living for either,
this beautiful city behind the ruby door,
with all its shimmering supplicants and priestesses
and sweets the size of bedrooms
and bedrooms the size of beds,
and little girls in vests like frightened rabbits
too exhausted now to not be good,
is no more than a rabbit-coloured jelly
spiked with splinters of glass that no one sees,
and no one's going to see,
because it's over;
is no more than a deep-frozen household
enjoying the tranquillity of cold.

Sky

For sky that slips between her thighs like oysters,
for sheets like seas,
for laps like seals,
thank You.
Thank You for inventing space, O Lord.

Blue

By being awake she can wake to the sound of a trumpet
and a girl in Detroit makes bras from the bodies of lobsters

and how can a thousand swifts not shine like knives
and nothing he said or did could bring her closer

and now he's gone she does it all the time
and now he's gone her time is like an aeroplane

where any time you want her you can find her
making the most of the sky by discovering blue.

PORTRAIT OF MY LOVER AS A HORSE

(2002)

Portrait of My Lover as an Angel

Nothing, as you know, would please me more
than if you were to find yourself in Heaven
standing on a cloud with nothing on
being measured by a large saint.

Portrait of My Lover's Arm

Your arm across my breast
is like a doll
nobody wants to cuddle
because it's headless.

Portrait of My Lover as Ash

My face
is like a face made of lips
being adored by a helpless drift of ash.

Portrait of My Lover with a Bag of Sweets

Whenever you think
I think I need a lover,
stop yourself.
I don't.
I need sweets.

Portrait of My Lover as a Bar of Soap

What I said I want
are lots of parrots
trampling on my back
like polo ponies
while you, O Lord,
congeal in the bathroom,
meekly getting used to being soap.

Portrait of My Lover as a Bay

To me,
you're tiny,
like a normal bay
being remembered by the open sea
where everything is blue,
and blue fields
go up and down
and up and down
like sorrow.

Portrait of My Lover as a Beetle

The look you give me is the sort of look
a beetle, Lord,
might give a large saint
who bicycles past across God's golden cumuli
and accidentally squishes
the beetle's foot.

Portrait of My Lover as a Blanket

You wet me
like a blanket made of throat
I drag across the bathroom
like a tail.

Portrait of My Lover as a Bride

You wait beside my bed
like a bride
who no longer pretends
to enjoy or understand anything.

Portrait of My Lover as a Bungalow

Find a quiet field
and lie down.
Surround yourself with roses
and a hedge.
And then, O Lord,
let me lie beside you
and stroke you
as I would
a dead lion.

Portrait of My Lover as a Butterfly

Inch yourself, O Lord,
into a leotard,
double-check your map,
adjust your wings,
and then, O Lord, before it is too late,
make your way at once into the mountains
to live a life of weightlessness
and rigour.

Portrait of My Lover in a Car

Lean against me, Lord,
like a lover
lying in a car in a lake
and leaning out against a shoal of minnows
that makes it hard, O Lord,
for him to know
if he is merely dead
or being worshipped.

Portrait of My Lover as a Cardigan

Wrap me in your arms
like a cardigan
made of the skins
of hundreds of knitted basset hounds
wrapping themselves around a small piglet.

Portrait of My Lover as a Chicken

If only you had been
a little chicken
living quietly
in a chicken-run
nobody, O Lord,
would have to tell you
they never even loved you anyway.

Portrait of My Lover with Chocolate Biscuits

My beautiful Lord
who comes rising out of the snow
with large bejewelled hands and chocolate biscuits
tells me in my dreams, as I in yours,
it's too late now for wanting to be held.

Portrait of My Lover as a Cockroach

You kiss me
like a scratchy little cockroach
scuttling across a concrete floor
in a wedding-dress.

Portrait of My Lover in a Cot

Air, my darling, is a giant ear
that never stops
pretending it can't hear.
So cry, my darling,
from your little cot;
cry to air,
your blue, your only mamma.

Portrait of My Lover with a Crochet Hook

Look down, O Lord,
and shower me with roses
as fragrant and as chunky, Lord, as cake;
look down, my love,
and with your little crochet hook
pick the sorrow from my brain
like crab.

Portrait of My Lover as a Crocodile

I wake to find you
stretched along my thigh –
as motionless and dozy
as a crocodile
that only ever eats semolina.

Portrait of My Lover as a Crow

Understudy light,
and when it's dark
fall asleep against my brown ear.

Portrait of My Lover as a Cushion

Be fat.
Grow laps.
Relax, O Lord,
and practise
being not only boneless
but serene.
Find a quiet sofa
and just sit there
doing nothing
like a square goose
that knows the only way
to be my lover
is actually to be
a small cushion.

Portrait of My Lover as a Dead Fish

Morning,
like an ice-pink cardigan
stiff with buttons made of wind and rain,
finds you floating
upside-down, O Lord,
and much too sick to know the word for *mercy*.

Portrait of My Lover as a Distant Mountain

How faint
you have become, O Lord,
like mist
where tiny mountain goats,
alert and numberless,
follow paths
that are three-quarters air.

Portrait of My Lover as a Dog

You lie in bed and watch me like a dog
watching deer
wander round the house.

Portrait of My Lover as a Doll

Curl your hair, Lord,
simplify your brain,
and burrow down
inside my towelling dressing-gown
where dolls, O Lord,
are treated to rough kisses
as warm and thick as slices of Peru.

Portrait of My Lover as a Donkey

Imagine I'm a carnival, O Lord.
Smell the flowers.
Stroke the giant moths.
Imagine I am swaying, Lord,
and stamping.
Imagine you're a rather bony donkey.

Portrait of My Lover as a Dredger

You groan beside me, Lord,
like a dredger
that groans with the weight of a thousand rock-hard dreams.

Portrait of My Lover as a Dress

Scream
like a dress, O Lord,
an unknown girl
with crimson lips
and legs like chicken bones
sticks a pair
of kitchen scissors into.

Portrait of My Lover as an Ear

I roam the world
in search of large beige ears
that comfort and uplift
the broken-hearted.

Portrait of My Lover as an Elephant

Welcome
to my serpentine hotel
where elephants exterminate small fish
by sucking them out of the fishtanks with their trunks
and squeezing them tighter and tighter until they die
and the glittering corpses catch in their ears like tiaras
that drop to the floor
where anyone running will skid
and sink without trace down a tunnel of endless night
where elephant babies are rocking themselves to sleep
while making peculiar little gasping noises.

Portrait of My Lover as the Emperor Wu

O let me be your baby,
Velveteen:
part your robes;
let me call you Wu.

Portrait of My Lover as an Engineer

You crawl towards me like an engineer
who works all night in dangerous passages
crying out for love
in ancient languages.

Portrait of My Lover's Eyes

Shadows spread across your eyes like wax
across small lakes tall women use as skating-rinks.

Portrait of My Lover's Face

Averse to the feel
of anything warmer
than ice,
your face,
O Lord,
is tinged,
like height,
with blue.

Portrait of My Lover as a Fall of Snow

Think snow, O Lord.
Think flurries of warm snow.
Sprinkle it across the land like tinsel;
like Cabbage Whites,
the sound of pillows,
sheep;
or like, O Lord, the whites of your sad eyes
if I dried them
and chopped them
and gave them small parachutes.

Portrait of My Lover as a Fish

On certain days
when all I do is swim
I entertain
a certain large fish
by teaching it
the fishes' word for *mercy*.

Portrait of My Lover as a Flower Arrangement

You're like a sort of resident flower-arrangement –
so handsome, Lord,
so stiff,
so *in the way*.

Portrait of My Lover as My Future Husband

Quaint lands of cocktails
lie in wait
like buckets
to drown tame wives
who marry
but won't purr.

Portrait of My Lover as a Glass of Water

Slither down my throat
like mountain passes
made of liquid rock
called perfect water
born to be the only one to satisfy
my large and small and medium-sized thirsts.

Portrait of My Lover as a Goat

You act as if there's no such thing as Ovaltine,
no such thing as wanting to be held.
You act as if it's even too much bother
to hold my hand.
You should have been a goat.

Portrait of My Lover as a Goose

Geese were made to paddle in small ponds
and eat warm mash
and live on citadels.
Geese were made, my darling,
to be eaten,
by candle-light.
You should have been a goose.

Portrait of My Lover as a Great Dane

You lean against me like a large dog
that doesn't want to know
it's far from home.

Portrait of My Lover as a Gun

Your lips, O Lord,
hairless
and indifferent,
rest against my temples
like a gun.

Portrait of My Lover as a Handbag

The shape you make, O Lord,
is handbag-shaped,
with lots of inner pockets
no one visits
where bits of fluff
mill around in darkness
like bits of God
in the process of not becoming.

Portrait of My Lover as a Hen

Couldn't you become a little hen
and live inside a coop
like Marlon Brando?
Wouldn't you enjoy a little house
where nothing happens
and you can't go wrong?

Portrait of My Lover as Hildegard of Bingen

O take yourself to Bingen
and a cell
with a narrow bed
and spectacular views of the sea
and a constant supply
of uplifting musical instruments
shaped like intestines
made of beaten gold.

Portrait of My Lover as a Holy Mother

You sit beside me
like a Holy Mother
sitting alone in the back of a limousine.

Portrait of My Lover as a Hook

Please invent a special kind of hook
to comfort and uplift the broken-hearted;
and please invent a special kind of sky
to which I can be carried
by the hook.

Portrait of My Lover as a Houseboat

How sweet and heavy, Lord, you lie,
like houseboats
rocking themselves
against old banks or barges.

Portrait of My Lover as an Iridescent Whale

Take your clothes off.
Fill your car with mud.
Then ease yourself into this large suit
whose thunderous and iridescent tail
will take you straight
to where desire began.

Portrait of My Lover as a Jug

Slip your clothes off, Lord,
and be my jug
for pouring cream
from cows
late coming home.

Portrait of My Lover as a Kitchenette

I would like to be married, O Lord,
to a kitchenette
whose overstated but misleading radiance
belies the fact
it's easy to maintain.

Portrait of My Lover as My Late Father's Suit

Flannel suits
with button-holes for eyes
follow me around
like small gods
that come from somewhere cold
that smells of fish
where nobody grows
and even the beds are small.

Portrait of My Lover as a Lollipop

You wait beside me
like a lollipop
aching for the warmth
of children's tongues.

Portrait of My Lover as a Lugworm

I'd like to be a very long tunnel.
I'd like to feel your cheeks against my sides.
I'd like to take you home to where the mud
can't remember why it's got no stones.

Portrait of My Lover as a Molehill or Molehills

What you really need
is a lullaby
to tunnel down inside your ears like moles
and turn you inside-out
like male molehills
that know exactly
how to be content.

Portrait of My Lover as a Motorway

You sleep beside me
like a motorway
where flat tin lorries
lie in warm rows
praising God
for letting them be stationary.

Portrait of My Lover's Mouth

Your mouth is like a mouthful of raw liver
whose crunchy flap's too icy to be sliced.

Portrait of My Lover as a Neapolitan Mastiff

Your only dreams, O Lord,
must be of me,
my little arms
so tight around your neck
you can't remember, Lord,
if you can move.

Portrait of My Lover as a Newt

Your tongue
inside my mouth
is like a newt
beside the penis
of a small baby.

Portrait of My Lover as a Nipple

O Lord and Master,
be my little ear,
an aligned and relaxed and resilient
little brown ear,
like a little brown troglodyte, Lord,
in a little brown cave;
or anything hidden,
anything modest like that,
anything mute,
that I can lie down beside,
and whisper to,
and feel calmed by, Lord;
like the ear of a calf,
or a freckled astronomer,
or a tea-bag or herb-bag or old-fashioned lavender-bag
slipped into little pouches of downy velvet;
I would like you, Lord, to be brown
and become blind:

I would like the world to be nothing but white wool,
with me in the middle,
as nothing but white lips:
I would like you, Lord, to become,
not an ear, like I said,
but a little brown nipple.
Can you manage that?

Portrait of My Lover as a Nose-Stud

Bring your flabby body
to my nose.
Drain it.
Dry it.
Whet it.
Punch it in.

Portrait of My Lover as an Omelette

O to be an undernourished spinster
standing at a window with an omelette
and gazing out
across a cul-de-sac
that shimmers
like the days before sin.

Portrait of My Lover as a Parrot

What used to hop around me like a parrot
has stuffed itself inside me with such force
I'm left with nothing, Lord,
but lumps of parrot-meat
and little mirrors with their pointless bells.

Portrait of My Lover as a Pearl

Reduce yourself,
O Lord,
to a pearl
made of nothing
but grains of polished sand
training themselves to become perfect spheres.

Portrait of My Lover as a Pig

Pigs are made to squelch in endless fields
like muddy chocs.
You should have been a pig.

Portrait of My Lover as a Pineapple Fritter

Wild lips
are biting into fruit
that oozes juice
through cracks
in batter jackets
that scratch my tongue
and tickle my fat cheeks
in a tinkling shower
of grease-encrusted sugar.

Portrait of My Lover as a Pool

May your lap, O Lord,
become a pool
for me to float around in
upside-down –
untouchable,
myopic
and repeatedly
blessing you
for having deliquesced.

Portrait of My Lover as a Poulterer

Your mouth is like a pair of rubber boots
that trample on my hair and smell of duck.

Portrait of My Lover as a Quince

Relax, my darling,
like the pear-shaped quince
that hangs in trees
not thinking about pears.

Portrait of My Lover as Real Snow

Real snow is beautiful
and murderous
and never sleeps
and never feels cold
and falls, O Lord,
we tell ourselves,
from Paradise,
to settle,
like white lips,
on small homes.

Portrait of My Lover as a Root

All you know is what a root knows
that only knows the language of perversity
and how to cling
and how to fear light.

Portrait of My Lover as a Saint

To qualify yourself as my lover
you need to go and get yourself beatified
then try again –
floating on a cloudlet,
and carrying a harp
or a lute.

Portrait of My Lover as a Saucepan

Saucepans spend the day being useful
and spend the night alone and upsidedown
dreaming of white coffee and pink fingers
without the need of needing to be loved.

Portrait of My Lover as My Second Husband

Smiles, Lord,
like fish the size of horses
swimming in and out of upstairs windows,
fail to make sense of who we are
standing here in our best clothes.

Portrait of My Lover as a Seraph

Stand, O Lord,
above my precipice,
then, leaning forward, beg the sky for wings.

Portrait of My Lover as My Servant

You prop yourself against me
like the servant
the poor demented empress
plied with lollipops
she kept inside her sleeves
like pet birds
ever since the fatal day
she murdered him.

Portrait of My Lover as a Shepherd

I wish you, Lord, a little hut on wheels;
I wish you snow;
I wish you rolling downs;
I wish you, Lord, a little snow-proof lover
for teaching how to graze
and how to bleat.

Portrait of My Lover as a Ship

I fear for you, O Lord.
The way you move.
As if you can't.
Like a great ship.

Portrait of My Lover as a Shrimp

You huddle on my sofa
like a shrimp
none of whose soft knees
can bear weight.

Portrait of My Lover's Skull

Whatever it is that makes the mothers of babies
know at once
when something's not quite right
makes me know you've got a little living-room
tucked inside your skull
where someone's ironing.

Portrait of My Lover as a Spoon

When you're next in Argentina, Lord,
can you get some DULCE DE LECHE for me?
To be gobbled up straight from the tin
with my little spoon
in my big dark house
where I'm pacing about, O Lord,
craving something sweet,
because sweetness and thickness
was where I went wrong, O Lord,
and you're more like ice
and all I need now is a plastic spoon for my jelly,
O all I need now is a white, moulded spoon
to hold in my hand
as I wait for my white milk jelly.
(You'll know it, O Lord, by the photograph of the cow
stretching around the tin like a white dachshund.)

Portrait of My Lover as a Strange Animal

Don't ask me why
but soon I started feeding it,
on caterpillars, chocolate drops, soft fruit –
anything as long as it was small.
Its mouth was as small and tight as a wedding-ring.
On moonlit nights it liked to watch the stars
and lean against me
like a giant jelly.
Then came the night I thought I heard it speak.
It said my name!
O Lord, it sounded beautiful!...
But of course by then I was out of my mind with exhaustion.
I had sunk to my knees in the sand I was so exhausted.
And the sacks I had carried contained only roots.
And as for my name –
it was only the sound of its gums
crunching the body
of its final wren.

Portrait of My Lover as a Sugar Mouse

Sugar mice are pink and white like you,
like juicy shrimp,
sweet mummified flamingoes;
like almonds dipped in tails,
crunchy thumbs;
sugared rose-buds,
frosted collies' noses;
baby voles in overcoats
too young,
too frivolous,
to know the word farewell;
like roast potatoes,
chopped and crystallised,
the hands of clocks
delighted to be free;

whittled, shrink-wrapped
hunch-backed sugar tongues:
I'd rather suck a nest of sugar mice
than you, O Lord.
So see what you can do.

Portrait of My Lover as a Suitcase

I want to live alone
with my suitcase,
a length of ribbon
and a tiny key –
as tiny
as the visions of eternity
brought to us
by faultless counter-tenors.

Portrait of My Lover as a Swan

A frozen lake
encrusted with dead swans
is not as stiff
as how I lie with you.

Portrait of My Lover as a Swimming-Pool

Be turquoise, Lord
and lean
and horizontal
and summon divers
in the dead of night
to sacrifice themselves
to needing air
and climbing silence
to inhabit height.

Portrait of My Lover as a Teapot

I'd like to have a lover like a teapot
that regularly plays the violin
with all the sweet indifference of dreams
to sleepy women in remote hotels.

Portrait of My Lover as a Tutu

Imagine you're as crunchy as white lettuces.
Imagine you're obsessed by skin-tight tights.
Imagine days investigating swanneries.
Imagine nights impersonating flight.
Imagine being mine,
and solving everything
by simply twirling round and being white.

Portrait of My Lover as an Upmarket Snack

Take the car
and go to Mexico
and sit in vats of honey
like a root
and when you're dead
I'll lay you out on tablecloths
and sell you to fat tourists
as rare fruit.

Portrait of My Lover as a Vale

Imagine you're a vale full of stones.
Imagine I can flood you with my tears.
Imagine I can swim across quite easily
to somewhere *made of algebra and fire*.

Portrait of My Lover as a Viburnum

You stand there looking bored
like a viburnum
pining for a road-side garden centre.

Portrait of My Lover as a Wardrobe

You watch me
like a wardrobe
in a sick-room
watching writhing women
without interest.

Portrait of My Lover as a Washing-Machine

Get white;
eat sheets;
and with your rubber throat
roar, O Lord,
for daring to be mine.

Portrait of My Lover with a Water Beetle

The more you weep
the more warm ponds there are
for me to whizz around in
like a water-beetle,
glinting meanly
like a hot bazaar.

Portrait of My Lover as a Wheelbarrow

I'll need a little shed to keep you in;
I'll need a coat;
I'll need a long night;
and then, O Lord,
with you to hold my hand,
I'll crawl into my little shed
and yowl.

Portrait of My Lover as a Wind-Sock

O to be the mistress of a wind-sock
in which the wandering wind
can rest its foot;
to billow in the sun
like bone-dry washing
the size and shape of an airborne
bungalow.

Portrait of My Lover as My Ex-Lover

I have fallen in love with the Gobi Desert, O Lord.
I have fallen in love with arms in the shape of hair.
I have fallen in love with lips like bible lands.
I have fallen in love, O Lord.
Wish me well.

Portrait of My Lover as a Yellow Camper Van

May you be undaunted and bright yellow,
may you hit the open road, O Lord;
may you have warm animals inside you
and strings of tinkly bells
dangling from you.

Portrait of My Lover as a Zebra

Grow a tail,
elongate your ears
and tiptoe through my garden
as a zebra –
a zebra who will take me out for rides
over the heath
to the sandman's private forest
where just to smell the pine-trees is enough,
to be dressed in a dress
embroidered with wild moths
the bedrooms of the married
are much too airless for;
where the sandy zebras' polished hooves on the pine-cones
crack like sound of abbots
cracking the spines of books
as gold and neat, my love,
as precious spectacles;
where the rabbits are striped
and the zebra's a friend of mine
and the eyes of the cats
are the colour of Vegemite jars:
O grant me, Lord, one night
beside a zebra,
one perfect sandy night
beside a zebra
that lets me rest my head against its neck.

LOU-LOU
(2004)

Ward 6
JUNE 2ND

They didn't have to touch us but they did.
They didn't have to bring us here
and wash us
and sit beside our pillows till the cry
of *Wakey, wakey, wakey, Little Ones!* –
'Little Ones' being us, enormous
blood-stained women
grunting on tin beds.

Night-room
JUNE 3RD

They didn't have to bring us here
and blind us
and lay us down
and leave us here like lumps
to rock inside this veil of white dots
we can't remember
how to understand.

Night-room
JUNE 12TH

People don't have faces anymore
and nothing here makes sense except pain
and everybody's here because they know
the only way to go is straight ahead
with nothing but a blanket
and the hush
of orifices opening and closing.

Night-room

JUNE 25TH

Leaving the vast and shimmering world behind me,
I find myself alone inside my hair
where, during the course of a million years or more,
tiny men with pointed hair like pins
come gliding in
in bead-encrusted ball-gowns.

Night-room

JUNE 28TH

Our beautiful hush
is blown apart
by Sister
whose rigid breasts,
so sumptuous,
and belligerent,
whose smell of wild cats
show no mercy;
whose knotted muscles
and unruly hips
have no respect
for our austere unhappiness;
Sister, who strikes fear into our hearts,
who'll stay beside us to the very end,
uninvited,
with her juicy lips.

Night-room

JUNE 28TH

Here she is again,
the tiny woman
who drags a little suitcase round my head
and never succeeds
in catching up with the man
who glides ahead
in a pair of gold-rimmed spectacles
refusing
to acknowledge her small tears.

Night-room

JUNE 29TH

Leaving the world of arms and legs behind me,
I rock inside the forest of my hair
that grows and grows
until it fills the room
and hides me in its hush like a sock.

Night-room

JUNE 30TH

I know they think I ought to want my mother
but all I really want are the plains
on which to gallop
on the grandest horse
far beyond the window where she's waving,
dressed in a tiny, tear-stained, sequinned cardigan
with lines on her forehead which mean I am breaking her heart.

Night-room
JULY 1ST

When Sister smiles
she makes us feel like chocolate
being licked and softened by a tongue
that spends its life seeking out sweet surfaces
with which to share
its love of licks and licking.

Night-room
JULY 2ND

We're here because we like to keep things simple.
We like to think of nothing but ourselves.
This place is here for us.
This place is ours.
The nurses are all ours.
The drugs are ours.
All we have to do is do nothing.
All we have to do is ache with joy.

Night-room
JULY 2ND

Sister re-arranges us like lilies
taken from dark homes
and carried here,
crushed and precious,
to be sanctified.

Night-room

JULY 3RD

Sweeter and more frightening
than the indolence
I used to take my clothes off and surrender to
our summer afternoons at the piggery
that shimmered in the heat
like a palace
that wanted me to know
it was preparing for me –
me,
its brutal and voluptuous queen
whose hooded court
withheld their secrets from her
a little while longer,
just a little,
and only distant squeaks in the heat
told her something somewhere was alive –
sweeter and more frightening is the indolence
that fills the sunless hospital like syrup,
an indolence disturbed from time to time
by the distant squeaks
of a patient before her doctor.

Night-room

JULY 4TH

We have long forgotten our houses and our homes,
our pretty clothes,
our little dogs on leads –
we're not that kind of woman anymore.
We spend our days doing this now.
We never stop.
We do it all the time.
We smell not of ourselves but of each other,
of rubber gloves and borrowed dressing-gowns,
of rubber doors
endlessly opening and closing
and offering up and taking away the instruments
that chart the brittle world
we're being groomed for.

269

Night-room

We refuse to think about anyone but ourselves
and what we want
and how to feel pain
and how to avoid being herded into the day-room
where somebody's playing *Whiter Shade of Pale*
over and over again as if to say
leave me alone
so we leave her alone in her corner,
pressed in tears against the Dansette.

Night-room
JULY 9TH

We take our time to answer her,
like aeroplanes
who don't know how to move
or where to go
or how to understand that all she longs for
is eyes that look her squarely in the eye.

Night-room
JULY 10TH

We hide in toilets
like large flightless birds
that Sister insists on driving into the day-room.

Night-room
JULY 11TH

She claps her hands like castanets imploring me,
beseeching me,
her *darling*,
to wake up.
Things become transparent.
Underfoot
transparent sand goes *darling darling darling.*

Night-room
JULY 12TH

We creep about the ward at night
with sleeping pills nestling
in the pockets of our dressing-gowns
like the motherless eggs
of a sort of mutated insect
that doesn't know or care about tomorrow.

Night-room
JULY 12TH

The fact is we are stubborn.
We admit that.
And Sister has to come on bended knee
and beg us to respond,
just a little.
Just for her.
She pouts her crimson lips
and stares into our faces like a helicopter.

Night-room

JULY 12TH

The tiny man
that slides across my brain
is leaning over slightly to one side
like someone who has somehow ruined something,
someone else's entire life, for example.

Night-room

JULY 12TH

We shuffle to the toilet with our toilet-bags,
we chew our hands,
we open up our veins,
but nothing will deflect her from her task
of driving us like froth into the dayroom
where easy chairs line up like solid rock.

Night-room

JULY 13TH

Her smell alone is like a terrible accident –
burning rubber,
burning hair,
white spirit,
and blankets piled high like big grey roses.
One little sniff and nothing else will do.
Everywhere she goes she is adored.
Everything she touches turns to gold.
My hair itself
she turns to solid gold.
And the sound of her shoes on the lino's like goats from the mountains
that climb on our laps and nibble our noses and hair.
We need her right up close so we can smell her.
Our rows of little nostrils are aching.

Night-room
JULY 14TH

No one is allowed to come near us
or ask us how we are
except Sister –
Sister with her stiffened ginger hair,
her skin-tight dress,
her eyes like flashing lights;
who knows without a doubt there burns inside us
a golden sea,
on which she sets forth.

Night-room
JULY 14TH

All we know is something dark is moving.
We lie in bed and let her swab our veins.
We lie in bed and let the starry night
with its glittering upside-down watch
keep watching over us.

Night-room
JULY 15TH

Only the grandest pilots of eternity
are good enough for us,
of darkest night.
Visitors who stand beside our lockers
fiddling with their handbags,
please –
just go.

Day-room

JULY 15TH

It's seven o'clock in the day-room, time for Sister
to rattle her nails like bunches of music-stands
and drive our troupes of *loved ones*
meekly home.

Night-room

JULY 17TH

Our hairy blankets
nuzzle us like goats
who think our breasts
would make a nice jam.

Night-room

JULY 20TH

She's come from the ends of the earth
to call us Sunshine –
or, *one*, to call us Sunshine and then, *two*,
to stay with us and be with us always.

Day-room

JULY 20TH

She likes to sit beside us in the day-room
designing the beautiful dresses with matching handbags
we're going to model
on the Big Day,
and offering cups of coffee
to those visitors
who are finding it almost impossible not to collapse.

Day-room

JULY 21ST

We sit in rows and grunt
like warm pigs
somebody's dressed in poodle- and peach-coloured slippers.

Night-room

JULY 21ST

My scream
expands
like ballrooms
into which
the duty-doctor tiptoes with his needle.

Night-room
JULY 21ST

Above my head
the fingers
like warm slugs
that trace the cabbage roses
of the eiderdown
are trying yet again to befriend me.

Night-room
JULY 21ST

In the bedrooms of the very sick
tranquillised and isolated brains
rise and fall
like plastic bags on water
that spend their time
adopting strange shapes.

Night-room
JULY 22ND

Remember we are graceless, vicious creatures,
terrified of even being looked at,
but even we,
because of her,
succumb.
Succumb to what?
I want to say *to love*.
All I want to talk about is *love*.
I want to say *I thought it was all over*.

Night-room

JULY 22ND

She fills the night with blood
like a mouth
filling up with blood
you can't swallow.

Night-room

JULY 23RD

My little bed
is like a private desert
where even the sand
is made of nothing but ears.

Night-room

JULY 23RD

The gold and silver days of being no one
are stripping us of bone
like soft fish.

Day-room

JULY 25TH

She's looking at my hair
as if to say
where do we begin
but I don't know.

Day-room

JULY 25TH

Our visitors go home
as soon as possible
but even there
they hear our low grunts.

In a Hedge

JULY 25TH

This hedge
is like a nice airy tent
where I can take my overdose
in peace,
hidden from the prying eyes of those
who've chosen not to kill themselves today;
who walk about the streets as if it's easy,
as if they were *born*
to wear big shoes and clothes.
Well, I prefer to sit it out down here,
letting ants play havoc with my hair –
what used to be my hair
before the nurses
turned it into a sort of perfumed hat.
They thought it would cheer me up but it hasn't.
It's like having something alive on top of my head...
in the dusk the tall bony trees
glare at me as if I should be going...

Corridor

JULY 26TH

The next thing I remember is the light,
and lying on a trolley like a horse,
and someone holding out a sherbet lemon,
and not being able to close my fingers round it.

278

Office
JULY 26TH

My distant feet
like someone else's cattle
seem to be content
not to move.

Office
JULY 26TH

All I do is stare
and say nothing
and think *I'm sorry*
and *I don't know*
and watch a patient from another ward
shuffle in and try and sell us lipstick.

Corridor
JULY 27TH

Nurses lead us
to and fro
like horses –
the most beautiful horses
Sister has every seen –
thoroughbreds,
with legs like icicles,
and veins
pink fingers
daily flick and tap.

Day-room
JULY 28TH

They come to bring us hope,
which we despise,
then Sister comes
and drives them out again,
and indolence returns
like shimmering mud.
No one moves.
We are no longer human.

Day-room
AUGUST 1ST

Our visitors look down at their toes
as if they are ashamed
of what they know:
that hopelessness takes care of everything,
easily,
even suffering.

Bathroom
AUGUST 2ND

It's nearly dawn,
and raining,
when she finds me
alone on the floor of the bathroom kneeling in water.

Night-room

AUGUST 3RD

She hurtles through the ward like a train
hurtling through a land of sacks and walls.

Night-room

AUGUST 4TH

I know we look like sacks
but we're not,
we suffer night and day –
because of her.
We slice our little violet-coloured wrists,
we spray the walls with blood –
because of her.
We long to hear her footsteps in the corridor,
to see again
her cheeks, her flaming hair,
to smell her sheathed and undulating body
whose rectitude
strikes fear into our hearts;
which disappears,
even as we smell it,
even as we stretch our arms towards it,
disappears,
without a word to anyone,
in order to pursue its secret destiny
far beyond this dark we grip like roots.
Her little dress is tight
like a spoon.
Underneath her dress she smells of onions
softening in butter over gas.

Night-room

AUGUST 6TH

Our blankets lie on top of us like sheep
too dim to know
how desperately we love them.

Day-room

AUGUST 10TH

Beyond the zoo-like sloth of the humiliated,
whose brains,
like roses,
are falling apart in our hair,
she offers us,
her loved ones,
without pity,
bonds we can't believe we are afraid of –
after all, we are afraid of nothing –
the hot and muscular bonds of a love
no other love or lover has prepared us for –
bonds or rays,
brutal like the sun.
She bursts onto the ward like the sun.
Everyday she is our only sunrise.
She squeezes smiles out of us like resin.

Day-room

AUGUST 11TH

She ventures forth across the rippling lino
like someone with the world's only map
might venture forth across an unknown sea,
bound for distant islands where her little ones
will dance about all day getting married.
But we prefer to dream about our deaths.
We dream about our deaths all the time.
We dream about the hand of the stranger
covering our face with a sheet.

Day-room

AUGUST 12TH

Her voice is like a clutch of wild parrots
screaming to the doctors
from her hair.
They rush upstairs
to touch it in her office –
the hair, the belt, the tights,
they touch it all.
As for us,
all we do is ache,
like lambs in yards who ache for warm ewes.

Night-room
AUGUST 12TH

Now I'm up
I go from bed to bed
stealing people's sweets
for the orderlies.

Office
AUGUST 14TH

It's all arranged.
I'm going off the ward,
now I'm *so much better*,
with a nurse.
Three of us are going down together,
taking money with us,
and a list.

In the Canteen
AUGUST 14TH

I think about it all the time now.
I think about the bridge above the river;
I think about the fish
and the boats
and music in the air
and captains dancing;
I think about exactly what it feels like
to feel so wet you feel too wet to breathe.

Corridor
AUGUST 14TH

The visitors avoid the numb arm
that swings against their woollen coats
like rubber
as Sister guides me
back towards the night-room
and lets me down
like freshly-slaughtered cattle
only she
is qualified to handle.

Side-room
AUGUST 15TH

She locks us in
like whippets made of glass
whose life depends on learning how to pine.
By 'us' I mean the patients in the side-rooms
abandoned to our various long nights.

Side-room
AUGUST 18TH

I'm on the floor
in someone else's dressing-gown
trying to go upstairs and tell the doctors
to interview the fish in charge of drowning.

Side-room

AUGUST 18TH

I'm lying on my bed among the living
like someone made of gold with human hair.
The visitors are scared of me.
They look
then turn around and hurry swiftly home,
leaving me alone with my breaths,
grey and soft,
like moles in a wood.

Side-room

AUGUST 18TH

She tucks us in our beds
like wild swans
who tried to fly indoors
and bruised themselves.

Side-room

AUGUST 19TH

She wraps us up
like victims of infanticide
then goes downstairs
to *throw away our clothes.*

Side-room
AUGUST 20TH

The doctor disappears
like a goods train
that travels through the night without stopping
or caring who is born or who dies.

O.T. Room
AUGUST 22ND

Are you feeling better? I don't know
Where do you come from, Poppet? I don't know.
Would you like a coffee? I don't know.
I don't know this is it.
This is kindness
leading me back to the lights of my long-lost home.

Side-room
AUGUST 30TH

We spend our days lying on our beds
drifting down what feel like brown rivers
that carry us away to lonely palaces
disintegrating into deafening seas.

Night-room

Look, she says,
aren't they beautiful?
and so we are –
although they disagree
as they draw the covers over the beautiful scars
of the beautiful necks they probably want to strangle.

Night-room
SEPTEMBER 2ND

We *will not have* stray people on our beds
asking how we are:
we are not better.
And nobody and nothing must distract us
from lying on our beds
like marsupials
refusing to acknowledge they've been born.

Bathroom
SEPTEMBER 3RD

Our glorious Sister,
like a summer day,
who never sleeps,
whose eyes are wide and scary,
who helps herself to people's grapes and chocolates
as they stare at their bedside lockers
and fall apart,
who is dragging a sleepy patient across the bathroom
to force her to open her eyes and admire my hair –
how sweet she smells,
how like an elephant
nibbling muffins in the afternoon.

Day-room

SEPTEMBER 3RD

We like the way her hair is stiff
like cacti.
We like the way she's ruthless and severe.
We like the way she likes us as we are
and not as people think we ought to be.
Visitors may wave.
We don't wave back.
We're far too busy sinking into a torpor
that allows neither eating nor sleeping,
far less waving.

Day-room

SEPTEMBER 3RD

How fat we are,
how abject,
like old frogs
squatting on the feet of their beloved.

Corridor

SEPTEMBER 4TH

She lets us be as ill as we want,
and when we start to panic
there she is,
ready to receive us,
like a runway
made of blood by God to serve the sky.

Night-room
SEPTEMBER 4TH

On quiet nights
we can hear the blood
pounding through her veins like God Himself –
God,
Who we refuse to be alarmed by,
Who all we really want's to be alone with,
and whisper to,
and find out where He's going,
in such a hurry,
in such strange disguises;
Who climbs into our beds and embraces us,
Who has no name,
Whose ears are soft and numberless,
Who rubs against our cheeks like Palaminos;
by Whom we are convinced we are adored.

Patients' Kitchen
SEPTEMBER 4TH

The doctors tiptoe primly past like dolls
but, once inside her room,
we hear them laughing –
throwing themselves against her desk and laughing.
No, *bellowing*, I mean, like dazzled bulls.

Night-room

SEPTEMBER 4TH

She breathes against my cheek
like a spoon
spooning something warm
into my brain
while far away
the days go by like barges
that have no heart
with which to know joy.

Office

SEPTEMBER 5TH

The bristly pigs
I loved to stuff with sandwiches
would press against my thighs
like the doctor pressed against me now,
but less discreetly.

Office

SEPTEMBER 5TH

The way I never speak
is like a mountainside
on whose white slopes
everyone is falling.

Office

SEPTEMBER 5TH

Sister is the only one whose touch
my skin can bear to be the object of.

Day-room

SEPTEMBER 6TH

She comes and stands beside us with that look
that means she loves us and she won't let go;
that means she loves us
of her own free will;
that means she has known and loved us
all our lives,
and is only keeping our promise,
as we must do –
and then she is gone,
and the ward sinks back into silence,
the silence of hearts that know *they can do no wrong*.

Night-room

SEPTEMBER 6TH

She's weaving in and out between our beds
like a lurcher with wings
in a sky full of cloud-dwelling rabbits
that can't resist not staying inside their clouds.

Day-room
SEPTEMBER 7TH

With chunky hair like handfuls of chopped jungle,
including chopped bromeliads and parrots,
she treats us like her tribe of *superbabies*
it's no use being less than ruthless with.

Day-room
SEPTEMBER 7TH

They smile at us
like they'd smile at sheep
they can't believe aren't bred
to smile back.

Night-room
SEPTEMBER 7TH

She's waving to us
from a long way off
like something waving
from a still lake
as if to tell us
as we fall asleep
never to forget
how much she loves us.

Night-room
SEPTEMBER 7TH

We dream of being ash inside white boxes
carried into offices by strangers
who carry in their other hands
our necklaces in paper bags
because we have no necks.

Side-room
SEPTEMBER 7TH

In the side-rooms
patients
like old horses
hang their heavy chocolate-coloured heads,
unaware
of rumours going round
that *razor-blades are on the ward again.*

Corridor
SEPTEMBER 9TH

Tiny married women
gripping handbags
are regularly led onto the ward
and offered bits of cake
like birds on leads.
They cry to go back home.
Well they can't.
They've got to learn to love it here,
like we do,
and think of it as their *new home.*

Day-room
SEPTEMBER 9TH

Welcome to the wonderland of dreams,
of evening meals in the afternoon,
of plenty of time for the tropical flowers to bloom
that bloom in the night in the heads of the tranquillised sick.

Day-room
SEPTEMBER 10TH

The woman sitting next to me is smiling.
Apparently she killed a baby once
but now she's as serene as a potato
who's never seen a baby;
only mud.

Day-room
SEPTEMBER 12TH

Whenever they see my visitor
touch my hand,
patients look away,
as if pained.

Night-room
SEPTEMBER 12TH

Because I've started feeling *so much better*
I tidy my bedside locker
with little scratching noises.

Side-room
SEPTEMBER 15TH

Dressed not in a nightdress
but a dress,
I've come to visit D. in the side-room.
Look at her!
She sparkles like red glass!
She wonders if I'm going *near an offie*.

Sister's Kitchen
SEPTEMBER 16TH

However much he sits in Sister's kitchen
and lets her dare him touch my puffed-up hand,
however much she makes me *look my prettiest*,
I want them both to know *I'm not moving*.

Toilet
SEPTEMBER 17TH

Someone new arrived in the night,
her sobbing like a beautiful wet dress
in whose blue skirts
she wanted to be rolled.
She's sobbing now.
She wants to go back home.
Her hair is like a curtain of sardines.

Day-room

SEPTEMBER 18TH

Happy days are days she'll start the day
designing the dresses she wants us all to be wearing –
though *how will she ever get married*,
she wants to know,
if we never stop keeping her rushing around like this?
We blink at her
like gravy boats
whose brains
can only process *sleepiness* and *heat*.

Patients' Kitchen

SEPTEMBER 19TH

Take her away!
Take her away please, nurse!
How dare she come here bleeding in my office!
She claps her hands,
and then we hear the sound
of high-heeled shoes coming staggering down to the day-room.

Side-room

SEPTEMBER 20TH

The very weak,
becalmed in their side-rooms,
look forward to those moments
when I treat them
to glimpses of the brightly-coloured pill collection
I spend my days amassing in a sock.

In the Lift
SEPTEMBER 21ST

The little sobbing creature known as Sunshine
is asking me to help her with her shoes
but loops of snot keep getting in the way
and anyway
she isn't wearing any.

In the Grounds
SEPTEMBER 23RD

We're being taken out for little walks
in order to persuade us
that it's possible
to go for little walks without despair.

Night-room
SEPTEMBER 24TH

Too proud to even deign to turn my head,
the nights she comes and stands above my bed
as if she's come from plateaux of the moon
to meet my eye and force me
to acknowledge her,
I nevertheless get tempted to peep.

Night-room
SEPTEMBER 24TH

How beautiful she is,
how like an eiderdown
whose satin roses
thrive on polished night
like spaniels
emerging from brown lakes
caked in mud
and spangled with bright fish.

Day-room
SEPTEMBER 25TH

The folds and swellings of her sun-tanned body
smell as if she's come direct from Heaven
to stand before me in her uniform
and tell the others
shuffling to the bathroom
to come and see how beautiful I am
sitting – no, *enthroned* – in the day-room
underneath my crown of hair-sprayed hair.

Corridor
SEPTEMBER 25TH

Hasty movement doesn't suit my hair
so walking to the room where they're waiting
is taking me much longer than they planned.

Stairwell

SEPTEMBER 26TH

The visitors are coming up the stairs
and walking back and forth
with little parcels
for those they have to smile at
and wave at
and hope and pray will one day be more normal.

Reception

SEPTEMBER 26TH

To the vision with tangerine eyebrows and rock-hard thighs
who appeared on the ward one night
when we least expected it
and proceeded to sail away
like the queen of night
down the rivers
and past the dark plantations
and out on the shimmering lakes of our hearts' desires;
who looked us in the eye as if she knew us,
as if it was time to go,
and we must get ready,
but who first demanded *everything* –
to her
we give not a word of thanks,
not a single smile,
as they lead us away to be normal,
hair-dos swaying.

RED ROSES
(2006)

This book is dedicated to the men I love

Nobody Stops Us

Nobody stops us
climbing into the cars
and heading off
towards a place they know
that's piled high
with bedding they can chew,
they can and do,
they chew and gobble everything,
they pin us to the bedding, chewing everything,
and screwing up our faces under chests
that curl with hairs like flies who've got no heads
and have to be content with their genitals.

They Like to Keep Us Well Battened Down

They like to keep us well battened down!
And when they're done
how tired we all are!
Suddenly it's all about forgiveness.
Suddenly it's all about love.
Together we remember to remember:
never go to sleep without a hug.
Never go to sleep!
It's not worth it.
Remember they've been waiting all their lives.
Pinch yourself.
Be vigilant
like lizards.
Terrible things happen when you sleep.

The Fact Is That It's Everywhere

The fact is that it's everywhere like gas.
We learn how not to sleep
and not to scream
and how to rush outside for gulps of air –
we gulp it down in lungsfull like great rocks!
The worst thing we can do is go to sleep.
Think of it as like an orange plain
where slender horses vanish in the heat
and screams from falling riders can be heard
vibrating on the edge of pain and pleasure.
We learn how not to move and not to breathe.
We learn to nip the pleasure in its bud;
we learn to nip the pleasure in its bud
like savage mothers with enormous teeth.

This Is What It's Like

This is what it's like when we're born.
This is how the night follows day,
this is how they smoulder in hot cars
and steadfastly refuse
to be forgivable,
this is how they grip their leather steering-wheels,
spattering the verges with hot mud.
Mothers are advised to keep quiet.
Babies are advised to die now.
They say you'll be all right but you won't.
Slip away while Jesus says you can.
Life is for experiencing Love
and people do.
Other people don't.
Slip away to Jesus while you can.

Our Softness Is Appalling

Our softness is appalling and untouchable,
it whimpers like the gowns of married men
that perish in the darkness of tall wardrobes
that stretches from our bedrooms to Japan
where every thing that happens happens softly
and love is like a bag of warm eyeballs
passed from hand to hand in the dark.

Terrible Things Happen When We Hope

Terrible things happen when we hope
and terrible things happen when we smile:
every smile betrays a little hope
and terrible things happen when we hope.

They Tell Us We Know Nothing

They tell us we know nothing but we do.
We know their voice;
we know what it will say.
We know it's near
and that it's full of love
and that this love is in the form of pain.

They Tell Us We Know Nothing But We Do

They tell us we know nothing but we do.
We know about brutality:
it's sweet.
It's private
and obscene
like mother's milk.
A little bit goes a long way.
(My little bit has lasted fifty years!)
Every day we do what we can.
We bottle it
and keep it in our larders,
tucked away.
Our luminous preserve!

Down Between Our Little Thighs

Down between our little thighs their mouths
chomp and chew us like the mouths of dogs
that chew their rubber toys beneath white stars
that can't believe how savagely they chomp.

They Stuff Our Mouths with Sausages

They stuff our mouth with sausages like sandwiches
and anyone who wriggles will be tickled
and wrapped and rolled in body-parts like bandages
and anyone who makes it through the night
shudders like a little gold toboggan
that's been flying over tree-tops in a snowdrift
that stretches from the end to the beginning
of somewhere where there's no one there to find us
and no one there to hunt the padded hunters
that tear at us and tear at us like bears.

It's Dark Between Our Thighs

It's dark between our thighs.
It's like a garden
where everything and everyone gets lost
and all night long they crawl and grunt like babies
down avenues of bruises' yellow roses.

They're Sick and Tired of All This Hanging Around

They're sick and tired of all this hanging around!
They need to just get on with it and do it,
they need to just get in there, and push,
and push and push our heads between their knees
and grip us till we fall apart like jelly
that nurses kindly spoon into a heap
on sheets as unfamiliar as lay-bys.

Our Private Parts

Our private parts aren't private at all!
Strangers like to cuddle them and smell them
and poke at them
like animals in cages
whose bottoms are as bald as ripe plums.

Underneath Our Pretty Summer Dresses

Underneath our pretty summer dresses
grow gardens of blue bruises like blue roses –
none of which understand anything!
They spend their lives trying to be pink
and dreaming of a god in perfect trousers.

They Always Think They're Right

They always think they're right,
and we are wrong,
which makes them very angry all the time,
stamping and crashing about,
while we are quiet –
wrong, but quiet –
which we prefer.

Terrible Things Happen in the Summer

Terrible things happen in the summer.
Terrible things happen when it's hot.
Terrible things happen in hot zoos
where kangaroos scritch and scratch their tails.
Terrible things happen when the sick
run upstairs expecting to be cuddled
and rocked in tender laps
and when they're not.

When They Walk Towards Us

When they walk toward us
darkness falls,
desolations falls,
as on a chicken farm:
they walk towards us
to extract our hearts
and freeze them in stacked blocks
they can saw.

Our Job Is to Forget We Are Human

Our job is to forget we are human.
Our job is to be calm as a vest.
Our job is to arrange for the arrival
of angels, by the coachload, in white vests.
Our job is to be dim and indestructible.
Our job is to be white as newborn vests.

They Ram Themselves with Thumps Between Our Thighs

They ram themselves with thumps between our thighs
and pour with sweat, like tipped-up Golden Syrup tins;
they jam themselves inside our leaky thighs
like mattresses inside abandoned mini-bars
where, deep within the vales of blue snow,
loneliness has built her secret palaces
that glitter like the tears of billionaires
nobody will ever find their way to:
the corridors are long,
the stairs are icy,
the lifts controlled by grubby-looking angels
who spend their days alone on distant landings
crushing heads between the closing doors.

We Ourselves Experience It As Lumps

We ourselves experience it as lumps
no one wants to have to think about,
far less understand,
far less touch –
except of course the tall fragrant doctor
whose slicing skills are famous
and unstoppable,
who slices here and there with gay abandon,
his blazing theatres throbbing with white light:
see his dainty plastic-coated fingers
skimming purple lumps into buckets
that overflow goodnaturedly on boots
as chunky as the paws of polar bears
that kill a person – bam! – just like that,
that kill to kill,
that kill and never stop,
that scrape and scoop until their paws are raw
and everything's gone red
like blood-red roses.

See the Flies

See the flies, delirious with joy,
on summer afternoons in tiled rooms
where roses part like thighs on polished sideboards
in houses we refuse to call our home;
see the flies, delirious with joy,
plunging blindly into fresh wounds.

Like Diners Pouring Syrup

Like diners pouring syrup through dark hallways
and treading it about on polished shoes
and spreading it about on caps and taps
and tiny moonlit sleepers like sardines,
like diners stumbling home
late at night,
they slap and stamp their swollen hands and feet –
listen.
Steady!
Hate will get us nowhere!
Hate will get us nowhere.
Don't we know that?
The diners' hands are handling us like gloves
full to bursting with reluctant syrup.

Love Is Like a Terrifying Angel

Love is like a terrifying angel.
We hate to hear its terrifying wings.
We hate to feel it crawling down our ears
like slugs in evening dresses down dark corridors
from which the sound of counting can be heard.

We Don't Know What It Is

We don't know what it is but this is it.
What we have to do is count to ten.
Count a little huddle of ten sheep.
Kneel by their sides.
It's OK.
Night will fall, bringing moths and sleep
and one by one the sheep will form a line
and tap their forty diamond-studded feet.
They'll tap and tap and tap and tap and tap.
Screaming cannot stop them nor can teeth.

We Learn to Stay at Home

We learn to stay at home
and stay well back
and creep along the corridors
like walls
and as we creep
we say what Fear says:
it says *placate*.
It says *placate placate*.

We Like to Do Our Best But We Can't

We like to do our best
but we can't.
We do our best to please them
but we don't.
We make mistakes again and again.
Why? Because we're stupid! We're so stupid
we feel homesick in our own homes!
We're homesick, and it hurts, but we're so stupid
we don't know what it is we're homesick *for*!
We snip and chop and swab and do our best
and all the time we feel sick at heart.
We shrink like shrimp inside our pretty dresses.
We shrink and rage inside our sticky hair.

We're Here to Look Our Best

We're here to look our best *and we do*.
We look our best even though it hurts.
It hurts so much it makes our hair fall out!
We shake with rage,
we grip the bars of buggies
and grip the tiny shoulders of thin children
we button up ferociously in coats.
Motherhood itself is like a coat!
Mothers have to wear them all the time,
even here, along this burning bench
that echoes with interminable sobbing.

We Learn to Marvel at the Golden Hair

We learn to marvel at the golden hair.
We learn to marvel at the knee-length arms
that like to feel their way to upstairs bedrooms
as white and soft as bedrooms made of flour.

Day and Night Don't Matter Any More

Day and night don't matter any more
and all that matters now is being cold.
Too bad we're cold.
Too bad it isn't easy.
Too bad our skin is turning blue with cold.
Isn't blue the colour of devotion?
And doesn't it get easier and easier?
Being this aware is kind of bliss!
Don't they know that?
Don't they know that vigilance
is always watching over us like hawks?

They Crash About Our Living-rooms

They crash about our living-rooms like aeroplanes
crushing trees and crashing into rocks
and strewing flowery mountainsides with passengers
whose sons will not be coming to collect them.

When We're Bored

When we're bored and lonely we go shopping!
We cross the pavement with our little bags
and make our way in haste to the station.
I wonder what will catch our eyes this time!
Perhaps a hat!
Perhaps a pair of shoes!
We're aiming for a bit of distraction!
We're aiming to forget the stubby fingers
riffling through our hairdos like the Pope
(even though he *is* the Pope) might ruffle
Our Lady's veil, to reach Our Lady's lips,
from which a stream of sunlight can be seen
lighting up a mattress where a man,
accompanied by several scowling women
whose skin is red
like roses in a rose-bowl,
enjoys his favourite way of being naked –
several of his favourite ways, in fact.

Look, a Golden Knee

Look, a golden knee can just be seen
being gripped and twisted by large hands
that work too hard to notice we are beautiful,
so beautiful that if we're touched we sing!

Overwork Is Just a Kind of Laziness

Overwork is just a kind of laziness
for people who enjoy being thin.
It twinkles on the foreheads of the meek
and by the afternoon a warm cascade
rumbles down their necks
like scarlet rocks.
Workers roll on workers with such diligence
everyone forgets how to stop!
They keep themselves alive by drinking coffee
and then by thinking thoughts of being dead
but when they find they really are dying
then they hear it call across the city,
across the golden halls –
that place called Home!
It's easy to be lazy when you're dead
but first they want to laze around at home!

We Think We Think They Love Us

We think we think they love us
but we don't.
We creep about unloveably
like insects
creeping about with half their legs torn off.

Like Glaciers Weighed Down By Being Cold

Like glaciers
weighed down by being cold
grinding frozen lakes
on lonely nights,
they grind us down,
they grind us without mercy:
our private parts respond like frozen shrimp
who can't respond
because they've got no sea.

We Sometimes Think They're Listening

We sometimes think they're listening
but they're not –
how *could* they be
when they've got no ears?
Their heads are blunt.
Blunt and thick like gloves.
Their brains are like the world's smallest wall.
Their hearts are like a wall made of icicles
dipped in concrete
so they never move:
concrete puts a stop to all movement
and with its creamy blankets brings peace.

Whack Us on the Head

Whack us on the head!
And again!
And watch the blood bubble in our hair
and watch our skin turn from pink to blue
and watch us going limp.
And again!
Don't they know our heads are hanging off?
No they don't.
They haven't a clue.

They Lie in Wait

They lie in wait for lips on which to binge –
and binge they do,
they binge until they drop,
they binge and bulge like little bloated puppies
that roll around the bedroom like their sins
(though only Jesus washes *those* away!)

They Told Us They Were Strong

They told us they were strong
and we believed them;
they told us they were kind,
but they weren't.
They told us that they loved us
but, my friend,
if they really loved us we would know!
Some of us fooled ourselves, briefly,
then fell apart,
like the perfect rose.

How Dangerous and Beautiful It Is

How dangerous and beautiful it is
to kneel in the dust at their feet.
Don't worry if we don't understand!
No one does!
This is what it's like!
This is what it's like to feel happy.
This is where they come in nice and close.
And this is where they like to make suggestions.
And this is where we slither to our knees.
What's the point of being upright anyhow?
It's safer to be stacked in special bays,
with blindfolds on, and rope between our legs.

Hush

Hush, there's someone coming,
grab a towel
and brush the lips and hair of sullen daughters
whose perfect man is actually a horse
on which to gallop to their heart's content
perched above the thundering flanks and buttocks.

We Are at the Mercy of Their Mercy

We are at the mercy of their mercy
and if you contradict us you are wrong.
We don't know what they do
but they do it.
They do it till they drown in it like bulls.

We May Not Have Their Valour and Their Beards

We may not have their valour and their beards
but what we've got instead is our shoes:
we step into our shoes as into chambers
lined with tongues that love to lick warm toe-nails!

If We Stop, Even for One Second

If we stop, even for one second,
diners will appear,
demanding roasts,
and light –
what light there is –
will start to fail
and now, my friends,
we need to slip away,
slip away and sit completely still
like someone with a zebra in her lap
who folds his brittle legs like polished handkerchiefs
and sleeps for ever,
dreaming of warm milk.

They Stride Across the Tarmac

They stride across the tarmac to brown aeroplanes
that have no room today or any day
for any woman with imperfect teeth,
imperfect ears or imperfect handbags,
whose families will discover them years later
rocking in the passages of hospitals.

We Want to Love Each Other

We want to love each other
but we can't.
We want to but it's hard
so we don't.
All we do is glare at the sky
whose yellow stars twinkle up above.
We glare at them until we can't go on.
We ask them to have mercy.
But they won't.
They blink their yellow blinks and sail on.

Everything

Everything and everybody glitters.
They glitter too,
like snails stuck with sand.
Every grain of dust and sand must glitter.
And, tucked up tight between our thighs, our hairs,
like filed rings, itch and glitter too.

Our Brains Are Like the Brains of Dried Peas

Our brains are like the brains of dried peas
that have no brains
and cannot disobey
and cannot understand how not to swell
as lips like juices make us into soup.

No one Comes

No one comes.
No one takes our hand.
Our dresses twitch
like dresses full of finches:
anyone approaching
must take care.

They Walk as if They're Stepping Over Bodies

They walk as if they're stepping over bodies;
they walk as if they're hated,
which they are;
they walk around like birds the size of overcoats
with hands like claws that pin us to the ground.

We're Living in a Place Where Prayer Begins

We're living in the place where prayer begins
but are our prayers beginning? No, they're not,
they're frozen on our lips like frozen whortleberries
stuck together in white frozen lumps.

We Stroke Our Necks

We stroke our necks,
we stroke each other's necks,
we stroke and scratch the necks and ears of horses
and go to sleep with tears in our eyes
and pillows in our mouths like lumps of concrete:
we can't believe that this is who we are!
We can't believe that this is how we live,
that every night is like a long journey
sharing nothing with a severed head.

They Like to Fill Us Up

They like to fill us up at top speed!
They like to fill us up to the brim!
They fill us up so full we tip and leak.
Our pubic hairs keep sticking to the sheet.
They fill us up and wish we'd go to hell
where we can be as sticky as we like.

Finally They Grunt

Finally they grunt
and roll over
and silence settles over us
like sorrow.

They Go to Work

They go to work, they work, they go back home
but something isn't right.
They don't know what.
As heavy plums gather in hot gardens
they gather in hot bars with laughing strangers
whose little necks they get to squeeze and fondle.

Be Like Us

Be like us!
Never smile.
Sob.
Sob for drips, a fuck, a cigarette,
Sob for Heaven like the sobbing sick,
Sob for nurses, sob for medication.
Could it be they love us?
I don't think so!
Give it up.
Give up everything.
To smile is to say *I am sick*.

This Is Not the Time to Start

This is not the time to start talking!
This is not the time to say we're suffering.
They haven't got all day, you know. *Quick quick!*
Shut your mouth or get the hell out.

They Take One Look

They take one look and have to look away!
O, wouldn't it be wise if they could take us
and pop us in a little drawer like lingerie,
smelling not of blood but summer meadows
where coloured flowers flower as expected
and coloured beetles live without love.
Love is like a large warm knife.
We keep it in a bag in our handbags.

Our Dream

Our dream is to design the perfect dress
whose icy sheath will grip us like a vice
and hold us steady till we freeze to death
and every little pore will be at rest
and golden hairs will rest from being warm.

When We Put Their Dinner Down

When we put their dinner down
they growl.
First they growl and then they start to bite.
They bite and chew anything in sight.
We do our best to keep their dishes full,
we fill them up again and again,
and even when they fall asleep at last
we rush and put their dinner down *again*!

They Must Of Course Be Fed Completely Separately

They must of course be fed completely separately
with separate knives and forks
at separate tables
that cannibals have carried day and night
up and down the tracks of rocky valleys
that yield neither virgins nor football.

First We Make Them Comfy

First we make them comfy on the sofa
and then we sit and watch them fall asleep ...
their coffee's getting cold on the coffee-table ...
O when they've got their shoes off they're so cute!

They Twiddle Us

They twiddle us as if we were machines.
They twiddle with our nipples and our noses.
They twiddle –
and when everyone's gone home
they fall on us and tear us apart!
It's not about forgiveness any more.
How can we forgive them when they're blameless?
They don't know what they're doing.
And they're cute.
Yes, we have to pacify them first –
by 'pacify' we mean remove the shoes
weighing down their feet like giant chops!
Once pacified and upsidedown, they're cute!

Every Night We Do Our Best To Love Them

Every night we do our best to love them
and some of us actually *do* love them!
They stay at home together in warm pairs
and snuggle up and watch the hours go by
like trays of strawberry jam and strawberry jelly.
And those who don't
look up to those who do
and marvel at them
as one might at fur
that seems to know exactly what it's doing.

Searching Searching

Searching, searching,
on our stiff red legs,
here we come,
searching yet again,
searching through the bedrooms and the boardrooms
for somebody to *run to*
and *cling to*;
searching till we drop
like amputees
who only want the night to bring them satin.

Every Night Imaginary Cows

Every night imaginary cows
come and stand beside us in our room
and gaze at us with disappointed eyes.
These are the cows of shame.
They will not budge.

Nobody Sees Them

Nobody sees them,
nobody hears the cars,
nobody finds the little place they know
where diners go to barbecue their cats;
nobody knows, nobody cares
how scared they are
of anything big and beautiful like night.

Just Because It Looks Too Dark

Just because it looks too dark to them
doesn't mean it looks too dark to us
and doesn't mean to say we won't go in.
If nothing else, they need to know we will.
They need to know we need to go right in
where beams of sun- and moonlight never seep
and nothing moves except the lack of light
becoming aware of a place where nothing falters
and nothing happens that we can't forgive.

They Come to Us To Swim

They come to us to swim
but they drown.
They come to us like horses to a lake
that glitters in the dazzling sun
like scissors,
they come to us and drown
like wild horses
drowning in the lakes of private palaces
with birds and fish entangled in their hair.

Leave Them

Leave them.
They must never be disturbed.
Our mothers hated everything about us
and so do they.
Never smile at them.

INDEX OF TITLES

332